THE COURSE INSTRUCTOR

THE  TIMES

THE COURSE INSPECTOR

A Guide to the Racecourses of Britain

Alan Lee

CollinsWillow

An Imprint of HarperCollins*Publishers*

First published in Great Britain in 2001
by CollinsWillow an imprint of
HarperCollins*Publishers* London

© Alan Lee 2001
© Illustrations Alwin Sampson 1984 and 2001

1 3 5 7 9 8 6 4 2

A CIP catalogue record for this book
is available from the British Library

The HarperCollins website address is:
www.**fire**and**water**.com

ISBN 0 00 712264 0

Printed and bound in Great Britain by
Omnia Books Ltd., Glasgow

CONTENTS

INTRODUCTION

It began in a Taunton traffic jam and ended in a boggy field beside the River Dee. It was an odyssey – as exhausting, eye-opening and endlessly rewarding as any other such lengthy journey – but this was an odyssey undertaken with a single purpose and a critical eye. The idea was to visit all 59 of Britain's racecourses, always on an active racing day, and to assess and compare their performances in customer care and spectator facilities.

For a little over a year, I was to behave as the racing equivalent of a hotel or restaurant inspector – and such was the breadth of the project that I had ample opportunity to judge plenty of them, too. Similar rules of engagement were to apply. I would arrive at each course unannounced and hopefully unrecognised (though, inevitably, this became more difficult as the series progressed), and I would experience each day as a paying spectator rather than a journalist. The ritual gripes and routine privileges of the press box were ignored – in fact, I seldom ventured through the doors – and all blandishments from alert course managements (ranging from 'you must come up to our box for a glass or two' to 'you will mention that we are planning to improve the car parks') were politely rebuffed. The judgement was specifically of the facility on the day, as any ordinary Joe would be able to view it, and did not include any analysis of the racing surface or the amenities for jockeys, owners and trainers.

The concept was driven by my belief that racing, for far too long, had taken its followers for granted. Many racecourses, probably the majority, had historically insulted the loyalty of patrons with ineptitude in the basic areas of access, car parking and the manners or staff, compounding it all with an infuriating take-it-or-leave-it approach to the accessories of a raceday – the racecard, viewing, shelter from bad weather, comfort of seats and toilets, and, of course, food and drink.

I had spent years visiting courses where the prevailing attitude seemed to be that it was a privilege for the paying spectator to be allowed in, and rather an irritant to have to serve them with anything beyond the most rudimentary items. Hence, racecards were black-and-white runners' sheets that utterly failed to inform or entertain beyond what could be gleaned from the morning newspapers; car parks were boggy fields presided over by crotchety stewards who would only smile if slipped a fiver for a favourable spot near the gates; bars were Dickensian hovels in which the stock was limited, the bitter a revolting keg brew, the wine served sour from the kind of screw-top bottle that even the better supermarkets had abandoned and the ice, cigars, smiles and civility non-existent. And still they seemed surprised when attendances were falling.

To constitute a vaguely scientific analysis, though, the courses had to be measured on the same criteria, by the same person, in as short a space of time as possible. I had been racing on 41 British courses before the series began but never, of course, looked at them in this judgemental way; the other 18 were to be new territory. In the first week of January 2000, Taunton was the initial port of call.

The Times agreed with my suggestion that the series should be called 'The Course Inspector' and went along with my notion that a written report on each course should be accompanied by a mark out of ten in each of ten categories chosen by me, thus generating an overall rating out of 100. Neither the editors nor I were initially convinced that the column could become a staple fixture in the Wednesday paper and yet – to my surprise and delight – it brought an unimagined response both within racing (which might have been anticipated) and from the wider sporting public (which could not have been). During the life of the series, I was struck both by the fervour with which regular racegoers received and debated my opinions and by the interest and enthusiasism it engendered in many people who did not habitually attend or even read about horseracing.

This proved two things. On a general basis, there is a huge appetite for consumer surveys, especially when they relate to such appealing subjects as racecourses in the countryside. More specifically, a great number of people plainly shared my concerns about the state of British racing as a leisure attraction within the highly competitive modern market. Anything that was seen to be drawing attention to the obvious deficiencies was to be welcomed.

That this was essentially one man's view did not strictly matter. Of course, I would have my personal prejudices and I would choose to air them – that was part of the attraction. The fact that I cannot abide the part of Yorkshire in which Doncaster racecourse has the misfortune to reside, yet find the environs of Ripon, in the same county, utterly enchanting, did not find favour with everybody and nor did I expect it to. Some insisted that the inclusion of a mark for 'scenery and surrounds' was unfair, in that a racecourse was not responsible for its position. I sympathised with the view but rejected it. The point of the exercise was to judge the level of enjoyment possible on a day at each course and, like it or not, a would-be spectator will arrive in better spirits for the drive over Cleeve Hill to Cheltenham than, for instance, the stultefying approach to Redcar through grim housing estates and past a cemetery and allotments.

If some of these ten marks were beyond certain courses, the remaining 90 were very definitely available to those whose efforts deserved them. Marking was undertaken with the size and wealth of the racecourse in mind – hence, just because Epsom could offer many more eating outlets than Exeter, for instance, it would not necessarily score higher for 'catering' – quality was the guiding principle. A rich racecourse would also be better equipped to produce thick, glossy and well-resourced racecards – and would be judged more harshly for failure – but this did not excuse even the smallest of tracks from making the effort to brighten their production. The better the card, the more advertising and sponsorship it was likely to attract to defray the costs – imagination and enterprise were the main missing ingredients in most places.

Here, though, as in certain other distinct areas, I found myself being progressively placated as the series continued. There were venues where standards remained generally low but only a handful appalled me, a few more deeply diappointed. Everywhere else, there were welcome signs that the alarm bells ringing through the racing industry had at last brought a positive, beneficial reaction. Importantly, the advances were not confined to the hypothetical premiership of racecourses.

From the remote and rural glories of Perth, the most northerly of British courses, down to the Devon duo of Exeter and Newton Abbot in the far south-west, I encountered a refreshingly transformed attitude that actually put customer care towards the head of the agenda. The installation of racecourse managers half the age of their predecessors has undoubtedly helped bring a touch of contemporary realism to the job and men such as Jonathan Garrett at Fontwell Park have been responsible for some enlightened developments. Young women, too, have entered the arena, bringing with them something far more substantial than mere fragrance. Lisa Hancock (now at Newmarket), Sally Iggulden at Beverley and Morag Gray at Hamilton Park all manage their courses with energy, initiative and a sensitivity to the importance of the little things – proper pathways, plentiful benches, tended flowerbeds and that once elusive smile at the entrance gates.

It was the Americans, of course, who coined the phrase 'the welcome experience' and it applies most pertinently to British racecourses. Embracing the value of such a concept has not been easy for some courses that seemed, traditionally, to instruct staff that anyone not obviously titled, monied or an officer in the armed forces should be delayed at the entrance as long as possible or, better still, deterred from coming racing at all.

Ascot was once the worst offender in this regard but, under the avuncular eye of the chief executive Douglas Erskine-Crum (a far more progressive man than the name might suggest), tremendous strides have been made to humanise its approach. Probably the best examples of making the spectator feel important as he enters the gates, though, are provided by the reception areas at Haydock Park, York and – most notable of the smaller courses – Beverley.

At the other end of the scale, those advancing past the graveyard flanking the entrance to Redcar should not expect to find anything more cheering beyond, while the gate arrangements at Worcester, in common with a good deal else at this most deplorably appointed course, are a shambles. I used to love Worcester, for its riverside setting, its cosy ambience – in fact for everything except the crawl through the oddly clogged town centre on a Saturday afternoon. Its deterioration is a scandal, and one that its owners – the vigorously acquisitive Arena Group – know they must address quickly.

As rail travel to the majority of courses outside the London area has become more unreliable and impractical, the provision of decent car parks is ever more imperative. An encouraging number of courses have improved in this regard, though not enough of those in a position to do so (in other words, not reliant on farm fields) have yet invested in the hard surfaces and marked spaces. Newmarket's Rowley Mile course, Kempton Park and Wolverhampton are outstanding, Worcester once again startlingly bad.

Queuing for an age to get into or out of the course car parks is another justifiable gripe of British racegoers and would not be tolerated overseas. Of course, in some places this is a product of the geography of the area and if we wish to maintain the varied heritage of our racing – and who doesn't? – very little can be done about it. Taunton springs to mind as a track with only one narrow road running past its entrances and no evident hope of achieving access from other directions. Too many courses, though, still decant every spectator on to a single inadequate exit road when it is not strictly necessary – Stratford and Sedgefield are prime offenders here – and tracks such as Wetherby and Uttoxeter that have acted to improve the dilemma are to be commended.

I set out believing that I would find only half a dozen racecards of the standard to which every course must aspire. Gratifyingly, I found more than twice that amount. The example being set by Towcester, Plumpton and Bangor shows what smaller courses can achieve with wit and marketing nous. Football programmes now sell routinely for £2 and racecards could follow suit without great rebellion, so long as the product merits it.

Communication is another area that courses have only slowly registered. Ever more now have permanent information desks and a heartening number acknowledge that the majority of racegoers appreciate an informative public address, especially if it includes pre- and post-race interviews with trainers and jockeys. Cheltenham and Kempton set the standard here, but the Devon courses and all those in the Northern Racing group owned by Sir Stanley Clarke are admirable.

Clarke, whose engagingly bluff manner conceals a demanding, pioneering spirit intolerant of inefficiency and indolence, has developed a formula at his racecourses that can easily be derided by those of cynical bent. There is green paint everywhere, band music to welcome the patrons, the staff wear identity badges, the loos are spotless and Stan marches around grinning toothily at everyone. It is called making people feel comfortable and important, and Clarke, in his own way, has done more than almost anyone to sweep away the reactionary instincts of racecourse management. Since acquiring the run-down wreck that was Brighton he has wrought a remarkable resurgence that can surely only be continued as the population of this vibrant and outgoing town begins to recognise the transformation.

Clarke now aims to do the same for two more deeply disappointing venues, Bath and Hereford, each of which would benefit from some sensitive rebuilding. In this department, the new or converted stands at Wetherby and Warwick scored highly in the survey, wheras Newbury's points tally would have been greater if its inspection had post-dated its recently built Tattersalls stand.

Food continues to be a concern, despite the best efforts of some innovative catering companies (Craven Gilpin in the north are excellent) and the recent, motivating Boursot awards for the best racecourse lunch. Viewing restaurants will continue to become more of a priority as even the smallest tracks with such a facility, such as Sedgefield, are proof of their potential. Lay on an edible lunch at a table overlooking the action and you will never have many empty seats on your hands – Wolverhampton, the only floodlit venue in the country, sells out its 400-seat viewing restaurant for every Saturday night fixture and it is sometimes difficult to obtain a table a month in advance. If this is not a lesson regarding the desires of the modern sportswatcher, I do not know what is, and it is greatly to be hoped that the London City project, aimed at producing a top-class contemporary facility for night racing in the capital, will receive the go-ahead following the ritual inquiries.

Not everyone has the time, money or inclination to spend most of a raceday consuming a three-course meal, and Haydock, Newbury and Kempton have all seen the light and installed bistros to accompany their main restaurants. At the more mundane level of eating, racecourses such as Ludlow, Exeter and Fontwell show the way with fresh sandwiches and cakes and filter coffee – the kind of things that ought to be basic requirements but were never previously acknowledged as such. I saw the nadir in the outlet at Newcastle with a blackboard menu offering as its choices 'pie and chips', 'pie and peas' or, the real treat, 'pie, peas and chips'.

Bars are being steadily improved to provide better atmosphere. York is pre-eminent, Wincanton and Hamilton offer style and variety. Racecourses in general, though, must guard against the Saturday invasions of heavy-drinking and offensively loud coach parties, a malaise especially evident at Haydock and Worcester.

Among the many letters I received during the run of the column, no subject attracted greater comment than the provision – or lack of it – of facilities for the disabled. Some courses have been extremely slow to recognise their responsibilities in this area.

An overriding impression, as the odyssey ended, was that racecourses have begun to realise they are not so much in competition with each other but with the myriad alternatives in sport and leisure facilities. With that knowledge, and with a more energetic style of management, they are moving the sport into enlightened areas and, at last, attracting a new audience.

British racing offers unrivalled variety, from the urban stadia of Sandown, Kempton and Doncaster to the rural idylls of Cartmel, Hexham and Kelso. The variety, though, should remain in location and atmosphere, never in standards. Finally, the message is getting through. If 'The Course Inspector' played even a small part in this breakthrough, it was an entirely worthwhile exercise, and one that should and will be repeated.

OVERALL RANKINGS

Course	Score	Ranking
York	82	1st
Cheltenham	81	2nd
Ascot	80	3rd =
Goodwood	80	3rd =
Haydock	79	5th
Sandown	78	6th
Chester	77	7th =
Kempton	77	7th =
Fontwell	76	9th =
Market Rasen	76	9th =
Wetherby	75	11th
Newmarket	74	12th =
Towcester	74	12th =
Uttoxeter	74	12th =
Wincanton	74	12th =
Hamilton	73	16th
Cartmel	72	17th =
Epsom	72	17th =
Exeter	72	17th =
Kelso	72	17th =

Course	Score	Ranking
Newbury	72	17th =
Warwick	72	17th =
Bangor	71	23rd =
Beverley	71	23rd =
Chepstow	71	23rd =
Lingfield	71	23rd =
Perth	71	23rd =
Ripon	71	23rd =
Brighton	70	29th =
Huntingdon	70	29th =
Pontefract	70	29th =
Wolverhampton	70	29th =
Fakenham	69	33rd =
Musselburgh	69	33rd =
Newton Abbot	69	33rd =
Nottingham	69	33rd =
Windsor	69	33rd =
Aintree	68	38th =
Carlisle	68	38th =
Salisbury	68	38th =

Course	Score	Ranking
Leicester	67	41st =
Newcastle	67	41st =
Thirsk	66	43rd
Ludlow	65	44th =
Plumpton	65	44th =
Bath	63	46th =
Doncaster	63	46th =
Southwell	63	46th =
Taunton	63	46th =
Catterick	62	50th =
Sedgefield	62	50th =
Hereford	61	52nd
Hexham	60	53rd =
Stratford	60	53rd =
Yarmouth	59	55th
Ayr	56	56th
Folkestone	55	57th
Redcar	54	58th
Worcester	52	59th

Perth

Musselburgh
Hamilton
Kelso
Ayr

Hexham
Newcastle
Carlisle   Sedgefield
Redcar
Cartmell   Catterick
Thirsk
Ripon
York
Wetherby
Beverley
Aintree   Pontefract
Doncaster
Haydock   Market Rasen
Chester   Southwell
Bangor   Uttoxeter   Nottingham   Fakenham
Wolverhampton   Leicester   Yarmouth
Ludlow   Warwick   Huntingdon
Worcester   Newmarket
Hereford   Stratford   Towcester
Chepstow   Cheltenham
Windsor   Kempton
Newbury   Ascot
Bath   Epson   Folkestone
Sandown   Lingfield
Salisbury   Goodwood   Plumpton
Taunton   Wincanton
Exeter   Brighton
Newton Abbot   Fontwell

0   50   100 miles

0   100   200   km

AINTREE

Venues known for staging one resounding event each year are exposed to harsh comparisons on their more mundane days. As the home of the Grand National, Aintree is uniquely privileged and uniquely damned.

More than Cheltenham, more even than Epsom, Aintree is pigeon-holed in the minds of the majority. It is the place they goggle at on

The County Stand is a reminder of Aintree's Victorian heritage.

1

Aintree itself may not be an attractive course but it has the National and the attention of millions at least once in the year.

the first Saturday in April and forget for the rest of the year. Many will be blithely unaware that any other racing takes place there, which makes it a peculiarly difficult course to judge.

Aintree is an institution, a cause for pilgrimage, and unless you happen to deplore all that the National stands for (and some do), it is the history that stimulates. Every step, every sight is evocative of the drama and sadnesses of the most tumultuous event of the racing year, which can make the staging of a handicap hurdle in October seem irrelevant if not heretic.

We are lucky to retain the course at all. For a tightrope decade, spanning the 1960s and 1970s, Mirabel Topham and Bill Davies were staple characters on the nightly news as the future of Aintree was debated as if it was a group of decayed buildings ripe for demolition.

Which, of course, is precisely what it was. As a spectator facility, Aintree was shamelessly seedy. It was the National track itself, extending across the urban wasteland of unlovely Merseyside, its challenges impossible to transplant authentically, that mobilised such protective passion. All of racing must applaud, for preservation has led to progress.

Aintree cannot be aesthetically pleasing; location would not allow it. Recent management teams, though, have been vigorous in upgrading both the racing and the amenities. The National meeting, as opposed to the race itself, has advanced annually and the three additional racedays – a springtime evening, an autumn Sunday and the November Saturday or Sunday featuring the Becher Chase – all serve a purpose by attracting different audiences.

Sunday was family day and Aintree did it well. True, the drive from the M57 (where more signs are needed outside National week) is so swamped by supermarkets, DIY centres and fast-food joints that Mum, Dad and 2.4 children may fall out terminally over the day's destination. Those who made it through the gates were rewarded with a decent show.

Car parks are improved in surface and organisation, though a bracing walk is necessary to get back to the stands. Here, if one can understand and forgive the pedantic security in April, the staff operation is outstanding. Sentry points are supervised by smiling men in green Aintree jackets, while a yellow-clad customer care team bustle about energetically.

On the basis that Aintree will attract plenty of racing newcomers, communication is equally impressive. The **racecard** is large, colourful and informative, while a paddock presenter conducts interviews and previews through the afternoon.

Children could hardly have been better entertained. There was a queue for the Grand National simulator, a following for the Aintree

Access 7
Car parking 6
Comfort and cleanliness 7
Scenery and surroundings ... 4
Staff attitude 9
Racecard and
communication 9
Having a bet 8
Catering 5
Bars 6
Viewing and shelter 7

Total (out of 100) **68**
Ranked joint 38th out of 59

Hotels, pubs and restaurants
☆☆

HOW TO GET THERE

By road: 5 miles north of
Liverpool alongside A59
Ormskirk road.
By rail: Aintree station adjoins
course.
Admission: Members £14;
Grand National prices fixed
annually.

Website: www.aintree.co.uk

to cater properly – and not only
on the dizzy days like the April
Friday, when the factories of the
north-west seem to disgorge a
motley but diverting army of
likely lads with lasses wearing
more make-up than clothes.

Sadly, even in the comfort that
contrasts so starkly with the
grimy relics around the historic
but inadequate winner's
enclosure, things could be better.
Food is unimaginative,
apparently proceeding on the
basis that nobody could want
more than a slab of meat in a
roll. Bars, other than the charming but crowded gallery that
looks out from the ancient

tours and a cheerfully crammed
model train circled the enclosures all day. Bravely, the hall of
the Queen Mother Stand was
given over to a crèche with
clowns and face-painting.

CATERING

With this and the other recently
built facility, the Princess Royal
Stand, Aintree now has the scope

County Stand, lack atmosphere and realism. With house champagne at £30 a bottle, no wonder there were no takers.

HOTELS, PUBS AND RESTAURANTS

Folk travel to Aintree with many things in mind – history, atmosphere and excitement high among them – but the experienced do not go in hope of a stylish hotel or winsome pub. In this area, there is no such thing. Leave aside the racecourse and Aintree is a disagreeably dour suburb of a city that has never been among my favourite stopping points. Liverpool has its devotees, though, and not all of them are pop music pilgrims. Jockeys, at least the young and lively ones, love to stay at the Thistle, Atlantic Tower or the Liverpool Moat House. My advice is to head north from Aintree, hug the coastal road past Formby and Birkdale, and bed down in stately Southport. The Royal Clifton is the English seaside to a T but boasts a surprisingly good restaurant, one of several in a town that also has pubby bars selling the prince of northern bitters, Timothy Taylor Landlord. Tree Tops Hotel, just outside Southport, is another possibility and Upholland Hall, off the M58 near Skelmersdale, is a rural haven with good food and a golf course. For a habitable pub with decent ambience and ale, try the Philharmonic, a Victorian gin palace in Hope Street, Liverpool, or head southeast from Aintree to the village of Daresbury, home to the Aintree chairman and the Ring o' Bells.

- **TOP TIP**: Avoid Liverpool and head for Southport.

TRACK DETAILS

The Grand National course is triangular, covers 2 miles, has spruce fences and incorporates a run-in of 494 yards. Inside is the Mildmay course, providing a circuit of 1 mile. It has birch fences.

5

ASCOT

Ascot takes itself seriously, as befits the flagship of British flat racing. Thankfully, it no longer takes itself quite so solemnly. The humourless austerity, habitually worn as a mask that deterred the uninitiated, let alone the unwashed, has softened into something approaching a smile of welcome.

Fear not. The Royal meeting has not turned into a free-for-all. Standards are maintained and bowler-hatted gatemen still rigorously

impose the demarcation lines, but there is no longer cause for those without a title, a foreign bank account or a morning suit to feel they have gatecrashed an exclusive private party.

Rather like Cheltenham, Ascot suffers from a misconception that racing takes place here in only one week each year and that only the privileged can attend. It is as keen to correct this as it has been to cultivate a more accessible image. Crowd figures, and their demographics, suggest it is succeeding.

The scale and age of the place create their own problems, however, and redevelopment plans, still at the preliminary stage but arguably ambitious, must address some of the deficiencies apparent during the crush of Royal week.

Ascot's forecourt will always be associated with the sing-song after the Royal Meeting.

One of the lions guarding the weighing-room at Ascot.

Change will be costly – £100 million is the likely figure – and possibly controversial. It may not be popular with Royal Enclosure patrons to move the parade ring and winner's enclosure, for instance, but the fact is that they are effectively out of bounds to the other 80 per cent of racegoers in Royal week, which is hardly a democratic selling point.

The boundaries of the Royal Enclosure are negotiated only by use of a long and busy subway – one of many archaic tunnels still in operation on the course – and this prevents most of the grandstand majority venturing to the lovely but distant paddock area. If Ascot genuinely wishes to be thought a modern sporting arena, something must be done.

Equally, the stand which so recently looked imposingly new is suddenly betraying its age. From the rear, indeed, it resembles a misguided 1960s' office block and Ascot's admirable efforts with flowers and paintbrushes can only be cosmetic. Viewing is good for flat racing but poor for jumping on the inside course.

Enough, though, of the negatives. The plus points begin with position, as the course is not only attractively wedged into Crown forestry land but also convenient. Traffic delays in Royal week cannot be avoided, but there is a wide choice of access roads from motorways to north and south, along with exemplary signs. **Car parks** are among the best in the country, clearly designated and properly marshalled.

The areas in which Ascot has made greatest strides are staffing, communication and catering. Of these, the most striking improvement is the attitude of the staff, who once seemed trained only in high-handedness. Now, they positively seek to help and there is also a well-sited information desk.

The **racecard** in Royal week has a minimalist cover and an absence of personality articles but it does boast jockeys' colours, guides to facilities and such useful features as a racing phrase book.

CATERING

An attractive new colour scheme reflects in blue signs around the course, replacing the forbidding black and white of old, and comfort levels are as good as can be expected amid huge crowds in ageing facilities. Bars, inside and out, are generally civilised, amply staffed and not outrageously priced – beer is £2.30 a pint and house champagne £27.

It goes without saying that one can eat anything from burgers to lobster at Ascot, but the sheer range and quality of the sustenance is impressive. Two innovations are trolleys carrying snacks and drinks around the concourses and the 'laptop' marquee that offers a picnic three-course meal for £12.95. Nothing, here, is languishing complacently in the past, which is exactly as it should be.

HOTELS, PUBS AND RESTAURANTS

The area has everything that money can buy – and there's the catch. Ascot and its environs reek of the rich list, and those of us looking for a hotel below £100 a night or a meal for two below half that price tend to be pitied and patronised. In the week of the Royal meeting it becomes an impossibility, the best of the smaller local hotels and guest houses being booked out from

TRACK DETAILS

Right-hand triangular course of 1 mile 6 furlongs, with ten fences per circuit, last half mainly uphill. Straight course (5–8 furlong races) uphill throughout.

HOW TO GET THERE

By road: On the A332, reached via M3 J3 from south and east, M4 J6 from north, M4 J10 and A329(M) from west.
By rail: Ascot station is 7 minutes' walk, with regular services from Waterloo, Guildford and Reading.
Admission: Members £17–£30, Tattersalls £12–£20, Silver Ring £6 (prices vary depending on meeting).

Website: www.ascot.co.uk

MARKS OUT OF TEN

Access 9
Car parking 9
Comfort and cleanliness 7
Scenery and surroundings ... 7
Staff attitude 8
Racecard and communication 8
Having a bet 8
Catering 10
Bars 7
Viewing and shelter 7

Total (out of 100) **80**
Ranked joint 3rd out of 59

Hotels, pubs and restaurants
☆☆☆

year to year, no matter what they charge. Rates at the Royal Berkshire and the Berystede – both convenient for the course and unarguably plush – are beyond average pockets and the best tip is to head for Stirrups Hotel at Maidens Green, near Bracknell or, better still, cross the M4 to Henley-on-Thames, where the Red Lion on the riverside is a restful retreat. Both have decent restaurants but gourmets will drive down the river to Bray, home of not just two top-class restaurants, the Waterside Inn and the Fat Duck, but also a splendid dining pub, the Fish. Other good pubs for a meal are the Rose and Crown at Winkfield and, even closer to the course, the charming and tucked-away Thatched Tavern at Cheapside, where the beer is by Brakspears and the wine list eclectic.

• **TOP TIP**: Thatched Tavern pub, Cheapside.

AYR

The first time, they say, is always the best – and it can also be the most deceptive. I went to Ayr for its Gold Cup meeting and excused the flaws as quirky. Returning on a Monday in January, when the crowd and the racing were diminished, other words sprang to mind: seedy, shabby and shiftless.

So the weather was lousy and the card second-rate, but British racing is sustained by routine and if courses give an uncaring impression on a mundane Monday, they are failing in their duty. Ayr is a big player, the stage for Scotland's biggest meetings, and it is a poor role model.

Ayr's Eglinton extension contrasts markedly to the older Club stand.

It is painful to denounce the place. Despite its remoteness from the southbound motorway system, it should have so much going for it. The coastline is spectacular, the area a mecca for golfers and Burns pilgrims, but the outlook from the course features dour, grey housing estates and a prominent supermarket. The aesthetic drawbacks do not end there.

Money may be tight but it would need little investment and energy to perform some straightforward smartening of facilities that border on the primitive. The stands are an unhappy mixed marriage of fading Edwardian and grotesque 1960s; colours are dowdy and paint peeling so needlessly that I almost wanted to do the job myself.

The concourse beneath the Eglinton Stand, dotted with fast-food stalls, a Dickensian sweet shop and a betting hall of depressing murk, is puddled and pitted and has the feel of a railway station in a destitute corner of Eastern Europe. Small wonder that spectators wander round with their heads down; the sensible have their eyes shut, too.

Ayr's average attendance dropped by 7 per cent in 1999 and new management achieved only a slight rally in 2000. There is a helpful enquiries desk in the main stand, but this is a rare sign of customer care amid complacent decay.

Communication is a classic failing. The **racecard** is dull and rudimentary and the public address booms and rattles through the stands, far louder than its content warrants. It would not take much

HOW TO GET THERE

By road: Just outside Ayr, the course can be reached via the A713 from the south, via A70 from the west or the A77 from the north.

By rail: Ayr station is 1 mile from the course; bus service operates from station to track.

Admission: Club stand £14–£27, grandstand £7–£10 (prices vary depending on meeting).

Website: www.ayr-racecourse.co.uk

Western House, Ayr, is an impressive and ornate building which is difficult to leave.

imagination to make both more entertaining and informative.

What are the positive points? You can find the course easily, signposted from the town's bypass, and the **car parks** are efficient, some even with tarmac. Club admission costs £14, twice as much as Tattersalls, but this is a course where the difference is stark.

CATERING

Buy a club badge and gain entrance to the elegant Western House, once the home of the clerk of the course but now a comfortable lodge with the air of a country house and the whiff of single malt. A three-course lunch costs about £15 and if there was a view of the racing, most members would never venture out.

The initiated will certainly avoid the cavernous Club Buffet in the Eglinton – where a request for filter coffee brought the cheering response, 'We've got Nescafé, that's better' – and the extraordinary wooden shack,

inaptly named after Be Friendly and redeemed only by the Scotch pies. Ayr changed its caterers recently and the newcomers can hardly fail to improve matters.

The track is flat and viewing of the racing unobstructed – best from the upper levels of the old stand, approached via staircases redolent of better days. Descend again to do battle in the handy but cramped betting ring, then seek out the pleasant champagne bar to spend £26 of the winnings.

Ayr has staged a televised Saturday meeting in February with Valentine's Day as the theme. It is a bright idea, with chocolates and flowers for the women, but any

13

Lothario seeking to woo his maiden should be warned. This is not an obviously romantic setting.

HOTELS, PUBS AND RESTAURANTS

Ayr houses a good hotel, several worthy restaurants and a neighbouring coastline of stunning views and world-class golf courses. Shame about the racecourse, really. Ignore the defects of the track facilities, though, and there is still much to savour about a trip here for one of the two main meetings – the Scottish National jumps programme in April and the Ayr Gold Cup in September. If you are not a golfer or cannot stretch the funds to the five-star Turnberry Hotel south of Ayr, Troon, just to the north and handy for Prestwick Airport, is still worth exploring – Lochgreen House one of several good hotels. In Ayr itself, pick of the bunch is the Fairfield House, where the rooms are comfortable, the bar buzzy and the restaurant outstanding. Fouters Bistro is a good dining alternative in town but you will look in vain for a decent pub.

- **TOP TIP:** Fairfield House Hotel.

TRACK DETAILS

The course is left-handed, 1.5 miles round, with nine fences and a 210-yard run-in.

MARKS OUT OF TEN

Access	6
Car parking	7
Comfort and cleanliness	4
Scenery and surroundings	6
Staff attitude	5
Racecard and communication	5
Having a bet	6
Catering	4
Bars	6
Viewing and shelter	7
Total (out of 100)	**56**

Ranked 56th out of 59

Hotels, pubs and restaurants
☆☆

BANGOR

Nowhere, in the panoply of British racing, is easier to deride from afar than Bangor-on-Dee. The one thing people tend to know is that it has no stands, which makes it sound risible. Then there is its location, which is not only remote but befuddling. It hardly knows whether it is in England or Wales and is so frequently confused with the other, coastal, Bangor that even trainers have been known to go there instead.

The majority of racegoers watch the finish from this angle, however, this is not necessarily the best view.

For my first visit in several years, I went suitably armed with map, wet-weather clothes and sense of humour. None was necessary. OK, it will never be the easiest place to find and the sun did shine for a change. But Bangor, albeit isolated and idiosyncratic, is no longer a racecourse to poke fun at.

A bypass around Whitchurch has made the drive from the south a shade less tortuous. Keep alert for the small racecourse signs off the A525, south of Wrexham, and if the day is kind, take pre-race refreshments in one of the two riverside pubs in an otherwise nondescript village.

Once inside, the most evident advances are stylish catering; atmospheric and well-staffed bars; improvements around the paddock and winner's enclosure; plenty of benches; and a remarkably good **racecard** with full colours and a distinctively designed cover. Strange to relate, once-rustic Bangor even has a decent website.

That it still has nothing resembling a grandstand is a matter of

local pride. The regulars in a crowd better than midway up the national attendance table believe it would spoil the ambience and I almost see their point.

The grass banks provide natural viewing but it is a curiosity that the vast majority watch the finish head-on rather than venturing round to the course enclosure for a better angle. Because of this, it is the only course where jockeys pass the post in eerie isolation, overlooked only by the judge's box and a few brave hearts 50 yards back.

The smug few, who pay a bargain £6 for this cheap area, can also view from their cars on banks generally less boggy than the main **car park**. Here, tractors are known to tow cars in as well as out, even when the river, which embraces the course, is behaving itself.

TRACK DETAILS

Left-handed triangle of around 1.5 miles with nine fences to a circuit and a 1 furlong run-in.

The setting of Bangor has few equals: on the left Althrey Farm adds to the rural atmosphere.

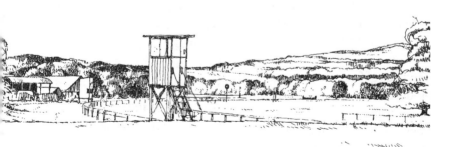

They have been racing here since 1860, when the memorably monikered Sir Watkin Williams-Wyn Hunt gave his blessing. Nine years later, a young jockey who was to go on to slightly better things rode his first winner here. His name was Fred Archer and he was 12 years old.

CATERING

It was only in 1970 that the course was properly enclosed – essential after a meeting was lost because of cows denuding the track of grass. Farms still stretch to the hilly horizons but the course itself has been modernised sensitively. There is a recently built weighing-room block and, of more customer interest, a splendid extension to the catering building. A spacious new restaurant is half given over to waitress-served tables and half to a self-service buffet with hot and cold carvery, excellent cakes and pastries and good coffee.

The same caterers service Hereford and Ludlow and set high standards of fresh cooking and produce. Their menus are extensive and staff are slick and smiling. A single reservation is that some prices are too high – a carvery bap needs to be sensationally good to justify charging £4.95.

Next door in the main food hall, well-filled rolls, burgers and soup provide food on the run and there is a cosy wine and seafood bar on the end of the block. A covered terrace outside has tables and chairs for alfresco

MARKS OUT OF TEN	
Access	5
Car parking	7
Comfort and cleanliness	8
Scenery and surroundings	8
Staff attitude	8
Racecard and communication	9
Having a bet	7
Catering	8
Bars	7
Viewing and shelter	4
Total (out of 100)	**71**
Ranked joint 23rd out of 59	

Hotels, pubs and restaurants
☆☆

dining at the summer meetings. A preserved black wooden hut, proclaiming itself the public bar, turns out to be far better than it looks. There is a pubby feel inside, with bar stools and wooden banquettes, and the one pity is that there is no real ale.

The most intriguing edifice, though, is the one 'private box', a tiny timber conservatory next to the horsewalk to the track. It has a balcony and bar, and I had an overwhelming desire to book it for the season.

HOTELS, PUBS AND RESTAURANTS

This is not a fashionable area for hotels or restaurants and, in racing terms, it is rather snootily overlooked by those from the main training centres, possibly because many of them can't find it. Settle in for a night before racing, though, and there is enough in the vicinity to keep body and soul content. In the village itself, the Cross Lanes Hotel bears three stars and contains a brasserie. For those in

HOW TO GET THERE

By road: 4 miles south-east of Wrexham on A525, then B5069.
By rail: Euston line to Wrexham General, then taxi to course.
Admission: Paddock £11, course £6.

Website: www.bangordee.co.uk

search of a pre-race pint, the Royal Oak and Buck House pubs are neighbours on the little river-front road. And that's it. For somewhere farther afield with all the creature comforts, travel ten miles east to Bickley Moss and stay overnight in the six-room Cholmondley Arms, next to the local castle. The food is good, the hand-pumped beer includes a local delight called Weetwood Old Dod and you might even see the local celebrity trainer, Ginger McCain.

• **TOP TIP**: Cholmondley Arms.

19

BATH

Think of Bath on a midsummer Saturday and every prospect pleases – well, it does if the aim is the Georgian city itself, cruising the lanes, cafès and winsome watering holes. Any fond illusion that the racecourse will match the splendour of its setting should be dismissed immediately.

It sits high above the town on Lansdown Hill, related by name but not appearance. It is a friendly place, likely to stir great loyalty among its clientele, but compared to the beauty at the foot of the hill it is startlingly shabby.

This is not an irredeemable course. There are treasures if you look hard enough but certain deficiencies – lazy racecard, unoriginal catering and crumbling paintwork – must be put down to lack of enterprise rather than simple, hamstrung poverty.

Bath can plead some mitigation, here, in the recent insecurity over its future. It has now passed into new ownership – the ubiquitous Stan Clarke – and what must be fervently hoped is that the new landlords will devote

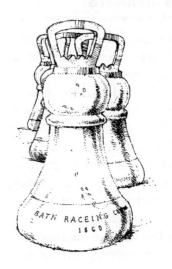

Bath's brass weights, with the unconventional spelling.

20

money and muscle to a worthy revival of a tarnished jewel.

Racing has been staged here since 1811, and it must have strained the horse-drawn carriages of old to climb the scenic and vertiginous approach roads. The course lies only 15 minutes off the M4 and is efficiently signposted, but if you are following a horsebox you must sit and suffer like a jockey trapped on the rail at Chester.

Car parking is free, plentiful and cleverly organised according to the direction from which you enter and wish to leave. Staff are relaxed and unobtrusive and, if the sun shines, the setting will make you spring eagerly from the car. Show restraint, for disappointment awaits.

At first inspection, the racecourse appears to comprise a series of cheap, dowdy and repellent buildings thrown casually together. That someone realised the error of these ways is belatedly evident in the appearance of a four-year-old stand in Georgian style alongside the faded original clubhouse, but these are consolations amid the architectural aberrations that insult one of Britain's loveliest cities.

Perhaps it will be better inside? The **racecard**, though, does not inspire confidence, offering nothing more enlightening than a runners and form sheet, and there is no discernible effort to inform or entertain on the public address. These are matters that do not require great financial clout, merely initiative.

CATERING

Anyone lured by the inviting lawn area into the notion that the Paddock Bar is the place for pre-race refreshments should reconsider. It is a shack with a corrugated roof and a concrete floor, its comfort levels those of the 1950s and its staple fare from the same confined vintage. The Tattersalls Bar is simply gloomy, but some relief comes in an attractive lounge on the first floor of the new stand.

Even here, though, the inhibitions of Bath are evident. The catering, while an improvement on the café in Tattersalls, proceeds on the basis that everyone wants a baguette. There is a small members' restaurant, from which some tables can view the racing, but the advice is to have an early lunch in Bath, then save money at the races by paying a fiver for the Silver Ring, which has a good viewing stand, plenty of bookmakers and food and drink no worse than that on offer further up the course.

The racing here is idiosyncratic, on a narrow, elongated oval where the runners are generally viewed either from the rear or head-on. It is a course for specialist horses, peopled by many devotees who deserve better. Those in the know will watch the races from an uncovered terrace atop the old members' stand that offers a panorama on glorious countryside. It is set so loftily it seems the closest thing to heaven in racing. Shame about what is beneath.

HOTELS, PUBS AND RESTAURANTS

It does not get much better than this. The racecourse is a disappointment but the Georgian city and its pastoral environs are an unalloyed delight. Sumptuous hotels and restaurants both serious and fun

TRACK DETAILS

Left-handed course of 1 mile 4 furlongs, with a straight uphill run-in of 4 furlongs and an elbow near the finish.

HOW TO GET THERE

By road: 3 miles north-west of Bath on A46, reached via M4 J18.
By rail: Paddington or Bristol to Bath; regular buses to course.
Admission: Club grandstand £14, Tattersalls £10, Silver Ring £5, centre course £2.

Website: No official website.

MARKS OUT OF TEN

Access 7
Car parking 8
Comfort and cleanliness 5
Scenery and surroundings ... 9
Staff attitude 7
Racecard and
communication 4
Having a bet 7
Catering 4
Bars 5
Viewing and shelter 7

Total (out of 100) 63
Ranked joint 46th out of 59

Hotels, pubs and restaurants
☆☆☆☆☆

can be mixed with some of the finest country pubs in the land. If only Bath had some two-day meetings, we would all have more of an excuse to linger. There are two five-star hotels in town, the Bath Spa and the Royal Crescent, but at a more affordable and no less enjoyable level the Queensberry in Russel Street, just above the Assembly Rooms, is a treasure – the rooms have space and style, and the basement restaurant (the Olive Tree) is among the best in Bath. Lansdown Grove and the re-opened Dukes are comfortable alternative hotels. Restaurants abound, and beware the plethora of tourist-trap dross; those worth visiting include the Moody Goose, the Hole in the Wall and, two miles west of town, the splendid Lettonie. Top pub in a cast of hundreds is worth a detour – the George at picture-postcard Norton St Philip, six miles south on the A36.

- **TOP TIP**: Queensberry Hotel and Olive Tree restaurant.

BEVERLEY

It must be 15 years since my previous visit to Beverley. It was a raw day in early spring, with a malicious wind whipping off the North Sea, and I found it such a stark, unwelcoming venue that I regarded my return as a duty bordering on an imposition. The experience, however, was one of the surprises of this racing odyssey, so pleasant that I briefly wondered if it was the same course.

This is an exposed spot when the East Riding weather turns nasty but the contrasting impression could not entirely be down to a benign evening. Beverley has been transformed.

There is the hand of a young, ambitious woman in control here now and Sally Iggulden, 24, has made an immediate impression. She inherited a much-improved infrastructure but the course now has a definite air of progress and punctiliousness, all the sharper in my senses for having visited its drab, dispirited neighbour, Redcar, the previous day.

This is another of those tracks that seem a long way from anywhere but turn out to be perfectly accessible. It is barely eight miles off the M62 and set on a leafy hillside with a view down to the

The view east from Beverley's course shows the tower of St Mary's and the twin towers of the Minster.

spires of the seventh-century minster, where Lewis Caroll, author of *Alice in Wonderland*, was once a curate.

Beverley's past is rooted in the wool and mill industries. Nowadays, it is a stylish market town, with cosy bistros and fashionable shops. I expected to take my leave gladly; instead, I departed wishing I had booked in for the night, in itself a credit to the atmosphere of the racecourse.

TRACK DETAILS

A right-handed oval track just over 1 mile 3 furlongs in extent. It is generally galloping in nature, although the run-in is only 2.5 furlongs long.

The lack of signs from the town is a negative and the **car park** – a huge, uneven field opposite the entrance – could benefit from some attention. Over the road, though, all is brisk and businesslike.

There is a smart, intimate entrance hall and the staff wear badges and uniforms – two simple but effective ways of achieving the

immediate aim of making the public feel important, rather than intimidated. Beverley's £1 **racecard** is not glossy or lavish but it does make an effort, numbering the races on page edges and devoting one page to course statistics and another to catering facilities. The public address is chatty, so we were told that 'Aunty Gladys, 96 years young, is here attending her first race meeting'.

CATERING

Gladys would surely have approved of the well-tended flowerbeds and the many benches around the paddock area. Everything here is neat and clean, exemplified by the Paddock Bar, part of the admirably designed weighing-room block opened in 1998. It stands at the top of the course and the first-floor bar has a large balcony which not only overlooks the winner's enclosure but offers a novel head-on view of the charge up the straight. Inside, the floors are carpeted, seating is ample and bitter at

HOW TO GET THERE

By road: Off A1079, 1 mile west of Beverley, or A1(M) and M62 J38, then via B1230 to Walkington.
By rail: Kings Cross to Beverley (change at Doncaster or Hull), then bus or taxi to course.
Admission: Club grandstand £15, Tattersalls £10, Silver Ring £3, course £2.
Website: www.thisishull.co.uk

£1.94 a pint is among the bargains of the racing circuit.

Best of all, this is not a members' area, so the price of a Tattersalls badge gains admission to the newest facility. The buffet food is good and fresh, especially the individual cottage pies at £2.95, and with the balcony vista taking in the preliminaries, the race, the celebrations and the minster below, why move?

Those who wish to trade up in the members' restaurant can peruse a menu in the entrance lobby, a thoughtful touch, while identical carvery baps can be had in both enclosures and a proper fish-and-chip shop fries its wares further down the course. Bars are not only cheap but attractive, none more so than the tiny creeper-clad cottage for owners, trainers and annual members.

Betting is not neglected here, with bookmakers pitched at both ends of the course to make the transactions more convenient,

and the sharp oval track is viewed easily from the steps of the stand. This is a course worth commending, and I doubt if I shall wait so long to go back again.

HOTELS, PUBS AND RESTAURANTS

In the kind of broodingly historic market town ideal for poets and TV thriller writers, there just has to be a pub of note. The White Horse in Hengate fits the bill, though to enter into the local spirit you must call it by its colloquial name, Nellies. This can feel a remote corner of Yorkshire, for all the convenience of the motorway network, but the Beverley Arms in the town centre is a decent, traditional hotel for an overnight stop and the surrounding villages, all trimly attractive, reward some inspection. Rowley Manor, a Georgian manor in Little Weighton, is a nice place to stay and the Manor House at Walkington has the bonus of a decent restaurant.

- **TOP TIP**: The White Horse pub.

MARKS OUT OF TEN

Access 6
Car parking 5
Comfort and cleanliness 7
Scenery and surroundings ... 7
Staff attitude 7
Racecard and
communication 7
Having a bet 8
Catering 7
Bars 9
Viewing and shelter 7

Total (out of 100) **71**
Ranked joint 23rd out of 59

Hotels, pubs and restaurants
☆☆

BRIGHTON

Given that the creator of an ideal racecourse for Brighton would never willingly start with the monument to neglect that still shamed the town two years ago, a remarkable makeover has happened up on Whitehawk Down. Graham Greene might have disapproved, regarding the place as far too respectable, but the majority will see it differently.

There must have been thousands of would-be racegoers in this vibrant town who neither dared nor cared to visit the evocative hovel

Brighton's stand has superb views over the sea.

immortalised by Greene in *Brighton Rock*. The ruthless race gangs had long ago moved on, but the course had never recovered its reputation, nor done anything about its increasingly shabby appearance.

Crowds had dwindled to a point where everyone knew everyone else and the merits of the place were propounded only by the feckless and foolishly faithful. Another year or two of apathetic management and Brighton would inevitably have gratified the campaigners for less racing by reducing our courses from 59 to 58.

It might be thought that Stan Clarke took an almighty risk when he bought this museum piece but recent history shows that he is a visionary in such matters. Racing in Brighton was assured once the takeover was signed. Crowds are rising steadily and night racing is back in a town that was made for it. Those who make the effort will come again.

Brighton always commanded a curious devotion and there are those who mutter that Clarke has stolen the soul from the track. What they mean is that he has banished its seediness, which was long overdue. Women and children come here now. Enough said.

Those familiar with Clarke's enterprises may sigh at more bright green paint, band music and beaming blazered gatemen with welcome badges, yet this is not so much a tired formula as a visibly successful one. Clarke has even cloned his beloved Uttoxeter with the design of the winner's enclosure and the conversion of

MARKS OUT OF TEN

Access	5
Car parking	5
Comfort and cleanliness	7
Scenery and surroundings	7
Staff attitude	7
Racecard and communication	9
Having a bet	7
Catering	8
Bars	8
Viewing and shelter	7

Total (out of 100) 70

Ranked joint 29th out of 59

Hotels, pubs and restaurants
☆☆☆

dilapidated shacks into smart, low-level hospitality suites and catering outlets.

The greatest change has been wrought inside the main stand, a structure opened in 1965 which can never have looked as good as it does today. Eighteen months ago this was still a shell, desolate inside and out, but the hallways are now bright and well equipped, equally welcoming for families as for committed punters.

CATERING

Newly fitted bars are well staffed and reasonably priced – wine is £2 a glass and, unusually, they sell champagne by the glass, too.

The main restaurant has an imaginative three-course menu for £25 but all the familiar Clarke catering is present, from the Nosebag's comfort food through to a seafood bar. Freshly filtered coffee features everywhere, a fine departure from those tracks which still think Tattersalls patrons can make do with the powdered stuff in plastic cups.

Communication is a strong point. The Brighton **racecard** is a snip for £1.50, interviews with trainers take place in the winner's enclosure and a staggering number of television screens around the public areas are enhanced by a giant screen in the members' bar.

The betting ring has been improved by a new tarmac surface and the bookmakers are set in a lively line. From the stand, there is a panorama of the sea, 400 feet below. Most important is the view of the finish line, which seems to have the crowd leaning over it as the runners complete the charge up the hill.

TRACK DETAILS

A left-handed U shape of about 12 furlongs; the straight runs sharply downhill before a climb from 2 furlongs. Like Epson, there is a camber towards the inside rail.

There is much still to be done here – how could there not be, when a mere £3 million has been spent so far? The seats in the stand need replacing, the **car parks** may need expansion and access signs to a difficult part of town must be improved. But Brighton, against all expectations, is thriving once more. Racing should raise a glass to that.

<table>
<tr><td>

HOW TO GET THERE

By road: East of town on the A27.
By rail: Brighton station, with a bus to the course.
Admission: Members £15, Tattersalls £10.

Website:
www.brighton-racecourse.co.uk

</td></tr>
</table>

HOTELS, PUBS AND RESTAURANTS

You don't have to be a Graham Greene devotee and enjoy seedy pubs but it certainly helps – most of the hostelries in the immediate vicinity retain a slightly shifty evocation of the *Brighton Rock* era. Brighton is a fun summer place, though, and you do not need to go far to find somewhere comfortable to stay or interesting to eat. Regency Square is a good place to start for small hotels that offer far better value than their swanky neighbours – try the Dove for personal service and make sure you get a sea-view room. The Grand with its 200 rooms lords it over the seafront but you will pay upwards of £150 for the pleasure. A mile away in Hove, the Courtlands in The Drive is a greatly improved and economical alternative. There is an eclectic choice of restaurants but most are aimed squarely at the kiss-me-quick brigade. For something more memorable, the Black Chapati is great fun if you ignore the prosaic backstreet setting. In Kemp Town, handy for the racecourse, One Paston Place serves modern French food of high quality.

• **TOP TIP**: One Paston Place.

CARLISLE

Sometimes, first impressions dictate the day but, just occasionally, they can prove rewardingly deceptive. Carlisle was such an exception. It had rained so much that the town's football ground was waterlogged and blown so hard that the racecourse had to close the damaged main stand. Yet the show was to go on and, at first, it was difficult to be glad.

Ample yellow signs had directed me the three miles from the M6, without touching even the industrial fringes of the town itself, and I was parked handily, if boggily, opposite the entrance. Even emerging from the car did not seem a good idea, let alone venturing inside this place of primitive, red-brick facade, set so high above the town that it is defenceless against the worst of weather.

There was a wind to cut holes in the hardiest constitution and skies full of animosity. I hardened my heart: there would be nobody here, the facilities would be derisory and the day would be purgatory. Wrong on all three counts.

The doorman apologised for having to take money for the **race-card** – only £1 and brightly designed – and the suggestion of being grateful for custom persisted. This is a cosy, clubby place where most spectators seem to know each other but strangers are made welcome nonetheless.

Do not go to Carlisle expecting luxury or careful formality. Such words are alien to these parts. Expect, instead, a rural track that maximises its resources and its community appeal, and does so with a smile. Expect weather-beaten faces and walking sticks and worries about cattle prices. Expect, in short, winter jumping at its earthiest.

Carlisle's racecourse buildings have always been distinctive and varied.

Carlisle actually races 11 months of the year, under both codes, but it is a jumping course in atmosphere and character. It attracts Fell farmers who probably consider the daunting five-furlong climb to the winning post no more than a gentle incline. This hill, best viewed head-on from the newer of the two rudimentary stands, distinguishes a course where hurdlers also gallop graphically past the rear windows of the weighing-room.

CATERING

The racing, then, can be a fine spectacle, even if the runners do vanish into a dip on the far side. Thankfully, it is not necessary to spend the rest of the day shelter-ing in a hovel perusing a choice of instant coffee or stale scotch eggs, and I soon felt ashamed of such unworthily low expectations.

True, the wine and coffee bar next to the paddock was not

33

what a city slicker might divine from the name, and it needed a sturdy chair and some patient hands to hold the door closed against the gale. Good home-made cakes, though, and more cheery greetings. Outside, there is an old-fashioned sweet stall and an ice-cream van doubling up with hot dogs.

Upstairs, in the members' dining room, Jonjo O'Neill was taking lunch with his American owner, Peter Thompson, and doubtless reminiscing about the jockeys' trip to Maryland on which the hitherto teetotal Jonjo discovered a taste for bourbon. Lunch is only £14.50 a head,

HOW TO GET THERE

By road: 3 miles from M6.
By rail: Bus operates from Carlisle station.
Admission: Members £12 (£14 weekend), grandstand and paddock £7.

Website:
www.carlisle-races.co.uk

some tables have a view of racing and the feel is that of a village fête.

The place to be, though, is the Lucius Bar downstairs, where smart and smiley staff serve whisky with half-pint chasers. There are cigars on show and a food counter with Yorkshireman's pie, at £2 a slice, the excellent speciality. But why serve bad wine from huge screw-top bottles?

Carlisle's efforts are best demonstrated by the recent repainting and papering in a building that would otherwise show the ravages of age, and by helpful maps of coursefacilities at convenient points. It is a course that recognises its weaknesses but

The Carlisle Racing Bells. Sir Loftus Bates revived the prize in the Carlisle Bell Handicap in 1922.

MARKS OUT OF TEN

Access 8
Car parking 6
Comfort and cleanliness 6
Scenery and surroundings ... 7
Staff attitude 9
Racecard and
communication 7
Having a bet 6
Catering 7
Bars 6
Viewing and shelter 5

Total (out of 100) **68**
Ranked joint 38th out of 59

Hotels, pubs and restaurants
☆☆☆

TRACK DETAILS

The course is 1 mile 5 furlongs round, right-handed, with a testing uphill finish. There are nine fences in a complete circuit.

Carlisle lifts the spirits. This is an area of rustic pubs, with a few gems among them, and some reasonable country hotels. If you want fine dining you must descend to the Lakes, though the Crosby Lodge Hotel, east of the town, offers a respected restaurant along with comfortable rooms. For convenience, the North Lakes Hotel off junction 40 of the M6 is hard to beat, but the more adventurous might divert west on the A66 to stop at the Pheasant in Bassenthwaite. Closer to Carlisle, the Duke's Head at Armathwaite and the Crown at Wetheral are renowned pubs with rooms.

plays powerfully to its strengths. It has come under the umbrella of Racecourse Holdings Trust, who recognise its potential.

HOTELS, PUBS AND RESTAURANTS

Just off the M6, with the churning conurbations of the north-west still fresh in the mind, the countryside around

• **TOP TIP:** Crosby Lodge Country House.

35

CARTMEL

If I have a regret about this consumer odyssey, it is the omission of a points category for that intangible essential of the sporting day out, atmosphere. Right, let's start again then.

Cartmel first, because it is a bank holiday Monday. Atmosphere? A resounding maximum. And nothing else matters.

To judge Cartmel by the same criteria as other, more orthodox racecourses is neither possible nor just. There is nowhere else like it, nowhere that even comes close. In its own way, it is the best and most successful of all British tracks, yet the virtues it parades so appealingly cannot be imitated elsewhere. The very idea is daft.

The view down the diagonal of Cartmel's circuit; in the background are the priory church and gatehouse.

For the purist, to whom racing means expensive thoroughbreds tested out on the straight mile at Newmarket, there may be no attraction in seeing moderate jumpers careering round a tiny Cumbrian village. Thankfully, though, the purist is a minority being. More than 21,000 came to be entertained at Cartmel on the Monday I visited, and many will be back. It becomes an addiction.

People come early to Cartmel – not just in time for the first race but straight after breakfast. Through the morning, the racecourse takes over the village square. The pubs all open and the Cavendish Arms, through the 14th-century gatehouse, starts a day-long barbecue, one of many that will continue inside the course long after racing has ended.

People do not decide to come here because the card looks competitive. For many, indeed, the racing is an intriguing incidental to the day out. Much like Royal Ascot, really, but translated to such rural informality that picnickers cover every square yard inside the running rail and impromptu football matches take place on the hurdles course.

A casual management, blessed with such a national treasure, might simply open the gates and let nature take its course. Cartmel, however, is not run by rustics and amateurs and the place is nourished with due care for the sensitive balance between standards and tradition.

The most daunting undertaking is to get the vast crowds in and out within the hours of daylight. This is achieved through a series of country lanes all carrying effective temporary signs. Inevitably, there is a bottleneck for those who enter through the village square but nobody seems in a great rush. The paddock **car park** tends to fill up well before racing but the solution is simply to open higher fields. One year soon, they will be parking on the fell top.

Gatemen wear Cartmel sweatshirts, flat caps and bucolic faces. The office staff are charming; on their window is pinned a notice offering casual labour to 'litterpickers' on the mornings after racing. Plenty must be needed to restore the place to the grazing green of its 360 non-racing days a year.

The **racecard** is glossy, informative and still only £1. Pre-race entertainment will usually feature terrier racing or some similar diversion, while the long lines of bookmakers start trading – and briskly – fully an hour before the first race.

CATERING

Not everyone brings a picnic, and Cartmel has expanded its catering operation with a square of marquees. The seafood and champagne tent has been joined by Chasers, serving a three-course lunch. There is also a snack tent.

Cartmel is full of curiosities. In centre course, amid the mayhem of a funfair and of stalls selling everything from bin-liners to bras and boxer shorts, the village cricket square, startlingly pristine, is fenced off. Back in the 'posh' paddock area (a steal at £10) the single stand has no roof. It is designed so that one can spin gently as the runners pass behind and then in front. Like the rest of this magical place, it is not designed for rain.

TRACK DETAILS

A tight, undulating left-handed circuit. There are six fences per circuit. The run-in of half a mile from the last fence is the longest in the country.

HOW TO GET THERE

By road: Via the M6 J36, then the A590.
By rail: To Carke in Cartmel and Grange-over-Sands.
Admission: Paddock £12, course £5.

Website: www.cartmel-steeplechases.co.uk

HOTELS, PUBS AND RESTAURANTS

Where to start is the problem here. The place is an institution, a monument to the fine things of English life. Cartmel is a unique racecourse in a beguiling part of England, and the loss of the three-day May meeting to foot-and-mouth disease in 2001 cast a blight on the spring for hundreds of people who make the pilgrimage every year. Cartmel itself has two fine country hotels – Aynsome Manor and Uplands – and it is the Lake District tradition that such hotels provide high-quality eating, albeit sometimes too formally for those who do not wish to mingle with fellow guests in the drawing-room before being seated as one. This can be avoided in the marvellous Old Vicarage at Witherslack, a short drive north, where the standards of accommodation, food, drink and serene peace are hard to beat. Of the many characterful pubs in the area, the 15th-century Cavendish, through the archway in the village square, must not be missed and the Masons Arms at Cartmel Fell is worth the meander through the lanes for a fabulous choice of beers, some home-brewed, excellent food and views to die for.

MARKS OUT OF TEN

Access 7
Car parking 6
Comfort and cleanliness 6
Scenery and surroundings .. 10
Staff attitude 8
Racecard and
communication 8
Having a bet 9
Catering 7
Bars 6
Viewing and shelter 5

Total (out of 100) 72
Ranked joint 17th out of 59

Hotels, pubs and restaurants
☆☆☆☆☆

• **TOP TIP:**
   The Old Vicarage, Witherslack.

39

CATTERICK

A colleague once said that the only thing that he could remember about a visit to Catterick was where he had parked his car. If he was there on a winter's day, with the wind gusting down the straight from the Lowryesque quarry, the preoccupation with a swift getaway was understandable. The management has taken to calling it 'the course with character', and deserves praise for imagination alone.

The plaudits, though, do not end there. Look hard enough and the efforts that have gone into improving facilities are clear. Catterick will never be the most naturally prepossessing of racecourses but it compensates by taking a pride in public areas.

If the course has an attractive aspect, it is best seen from the **car park**. Linger in the vehicle, conveniently docked across the road from the main gate, and it is easy to believe that the view of the

The Bridge House Inn can be seen beyond the stands, an ideal place for refreshment.

ancient river bridge loomed over by the Bridge House Inn might be quite agreeable on a blue summer day. There is ample opportunity, for this is a busy course, its 27 meetings spread across every month bar May.

Catterick first staged racing in 1783 but the main grandstand was built in 1926, three years after the nearby army camp opened to recruits. The A1 is almost audible from the course and, despite a shortage of signposts, even the logistically challenged would be hard put to miss it. Of the nine Yorkshire tracks, this is the smallest and, considering the proximity of Richmond's cobbled streets and Wensleydale's rustic charm, the most aesthetically deflating.

CATERING

Some of the staff are gruff, others quaint. In the subterranean toilets, all chipped marble and noisy pipes, an ancient attendant sits with an optimistic ashtray for tips and one could almost believe he was there when the stand opened. The time-warp feel is more positive in some areas, and the single-storey Paddock Bar and dining room has charm and substance.

An ambitious lunch menu includes seafood bouillabaisse (£7.15) or, more exotically, 'breast of lamb stuffed with a lamb and fruit forcemeat, slow cooked and served with a spicy Moroccan lentil sauce', which is hardly flat-cap food, even at a reasonable £6.95. The Club Bar serves home-made giant Yorkshire puddings with various fillings (£2.00 to £3.45) but, perversely, they are not available in the new, neatly carpeted bar for non-members.

Back a winner here, or better still own one, and you can celebrate with a semblance of style. Sixteen different

MARKS OUT OF TEN

Access 7
Car parking 7
Comfort and cleanliness 8
Scenery and surroundings ... 4
Staff attitude 6
Racecard and
communication 3
Having a bet 6
Catering 7
Bars 7
Viewing and shelter 7

Total (out of 100) 62
Ranked joint 50th out of 59

Hotels, pubs and restaurants
☆

champagnes are available (£22 to £42) and cigars are on display. The bars, which serve John Smith's and Guinness on tap, pass one test by having buckets of ice but fail another by serving revolting white wine out of screw-top bottles and not even keeping it cold. Pubs have learnt the market for decent wine by the glass; why are racecourses so slow?

There is nothing very easy on

HOW TO GET THERE

By road: Via the A1, close to the junction of the A66 (Scotch Corner).
By rail: To Darlington or Northallerton. Bus service to course.
Admission: Club stand £13, Tattersalls £9, course £2.50.

Website: www.catterick.com

the eye in the view from the stand but it does offer decent shelter and a panorama of this tight left-handed track with its gentle undulations. Even on a bleak January day, there were 30 bookmakers in a barely adequate betting ring; there is also a Tote shop with a dilapidated hovel of a bar attached.

Catterick should do better with its **racecard**, which looks as if it has been turned out on a home printer and is lacking in any editorial, and the public address is sketchy and uninformative. Back to the Paddock Bar, then. Or, better still, the car park.

HOTELS, PUBS AND RESTAURANTS

There is something irredeemably bleak about Catterick and this is reflected in the local choice of hostelries. Across the A1, Richmond, with its cobbles and market square, is far more attractive and the King's Head is a reasonable base. Middleham, which houses a crop of training yards and a good dining pub in the White Swan, is not far away but the best choice locally is the Blue Lion in the tiny village of East Witton – a well-run pub with decent rooms, Black Sheep ale and quite outstanding food and wine. Ignore Catterick – unless you simply must have a pint in the Bridge House Inn opposite the course – and head west.

- **TOP TIP**: Blue Lion at East Witton.

TRACK DETAILS

A left-handed oval of about 1.25 miles with eight fences in a complete circuit.

43

CHELTENHAM

The key to Cheltenham's phenomenal success is that the place never stands still. Year after year, innovations appear to make the flustered customer feel more comfortable. The one that took the eye on my visit was the chemist's shop.

It opened for business next to that other essential Festival precaution – the lost-property office – and its shelves were piled high with headache cures. Edward Gillespie, ringmaster of Cheltenham, must be slowing down; why had he not thought of this before?

Cheltenham has taken giant strides in recent years and, remarkably, there are those who resent it fiercely. Mostly these are the senior members, who jealously recall when they enjoyed the run of the place and the facilities were a cross between a country club and the Heythrop point-to-point.

They feel Gillespie, in taking Cheltenham to the people and making it a thoroughly modern stadium, has reduced their privileges, spoiled their private party. For the majority, however, progress has been positive and pleasing. Of course, the Festival is

---

The Arkle Bar is still the best place for those needing a drink.

During WWI Cheltenham racecourse was a hospital. Its recreation-room fireplace has its bricks pitted through billiard-cue chalking.

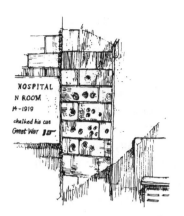

crazy; some of the buildings are dark and dated and there will never be enough toilets or bars or bookmakers. The brutal truth is that the fragile, impatient or claustrophobic should not come.

CATERING

On the site where the local vicar had the original stand burnt to the ground in 1830, new structures have been seamlessly stitched on to old. The panoramic restaurant, beyond the winning line, is one of the most impressive in Britain, if you are quick and rich enough to acquire a table.

The rest of us need not starve. There are almost 100 food outlets during Festival week, with no fewer than six camped around the gates that opened precisely at 10.30am to whoops of pent-up enthusiasm from punters, some showing a turn of foot they had not raised in years.

In Ireland recently, someone earnestly asked me why Cheltenham only stages racing three days a year. This is a common misconception – there are even those in the town unaware that what they still call 'Gold Cup week' is only part of a 15-day portfolio of jump racing.

The rest, all decent quality, can be watched at leisure and in luxury, for Cheltenham's standards are not allowed to drop. It is a daunting benchmark they have set themselves but lapses are few. The course is now more easily accessed, with efficient signposting, additional exit gates and **car parks** – enough for 14,000 vehicles – generally much better surfaced than in the old days of muddy misery.

The staff are under pressure and might be brisk rather than charming but the operation they run is remarkably smooth, from those who check badges coming in to the army that cleans up tons of litter each night – almost a spectacle in itself.

Racecards are £2 all year and, to judge by the number of adverts within, the Festival cards must make a fortune. The design is good, with clear and helpful guides to facilities, while the news and interviews, conducted in the winner's enclosure and broadcast over the public address, add impressively to the showtime feel.

The betting ring used to be hopelessly inadequate in Festival week; now, through extensions and movements of some bookies elsewhere – even, misguidedly, to a crowded thoroughfare – it is merely inadequate.

Best spot for a drink is the Arkle Bar, while those needing solids should seek out Barrie

Prestbury Park, Cheltenham: from the back section a good view of the stands on the rising home straight.

Cope's new seafood counter in the Golden Miller Bar. Get there early, grab a table and order baked salmon and prawns at £15 a plate. Then walk outside for the finest sight in racing, the views across to Cleeve Hill soothing the pain of the first losing bet.

The tented village is bigger and better than ever. Someone is selling See More Business wine, class in a bottle at £20. The most optimistic addition is a small, fenced area called the Still Place, which invites you to sit quietly for two minutes. No takers, last time I looked.

TRACK DETAILS

There are two left-hand courses at Cheltenham: the Old Course and the New Course. Both are testing in nature with nine fences to a circuit.

HOTELS, PUBS AND RESTAURANTS

Like Cartmel, though on a grander scale, Cheltenham offers something for every taste. It may be intolerably packed during Festival week – hugely lamented in 2001 – but for the remaining meetings the choice is almost overwhelming. Regency Montpellier has the lively bars, of which the Montpellier wine bar is much the most stylish. Pubs close to the course include the cosy Sudeley Arms in Portland Square, but the best pubs are to be found in the surrounding villages. The Green Dragon at Cowley, Kilkeney Inn near Andoversford and the Bathurst

HOW TO GET THERE

By road: 1 mile north of town on A435. Can be reached by leaving the M5 at J9, J10 or J11.
By rail: To Cheltenham Spa. A bus service runs from the station.
Admission: Club £14–£60, Tattersalls £14–£30, Courage Best £5–£15 (prices vary depending on meeting).

Website: www.cheltenham.co.uk

MARKS OUT OF TEN

Access	8
Car parking	9
Comfort and cleanliness	8
Scenery and surroundings	10
Staff attitude	8
Racecard and communication	8
Having a bet	6
Catering	8
Bars	7
Viewing and shelter	9

Total (out of 100) **81**
Ranked 2nd out of 59

Hotels, pubs and restaurants
☆☆☆☆☆

Arms on the Cirencester road at North Cerney all combine the vital ingredients of good wine, beer, food and atmosphere. Town-centre restaurants abound – Champignon Sauvage in Suffolk Road remains the best for fine dining and Petit Blanc in Montpellier the buzziest on a daily basis, but two excellent newcomers are the slick Italian-influenced Café Paradiso in the Hotel Kandinsky in Montpellier and Lumiere – minimalist décor but great food and wine list – in a Georgian terrace just off the Promenade. The Kandinsky is now a fun place to stay, the Queen's still looms large from the head of town and On the Park, 400 yards from the racecourse opposite Pittville Park, has 12 opulent rooms and a fine restaurant.

- **TOP TIP**: Hotel Kandinsky and Café Paradiso.

CHEPSTOW

One gauge of a good racecourse is the number of times it is spoken of with affection. Strain the ears all you like but you will not hear many eulogies about Folkestone, for instance, or Ayr as a favourite track. Chepstow, by contrast, creates a clamour of devotion and it is not difficult to see why.

If beauty were the sole criterion, Chepstow would have few peers. The town itself is attractive, with its castle and river, but the course is bucolic bliss. This would be no more than superficial cachet if the

A view from the parade ring at Chepstow.

Piercefield was laid out in 1753, but it was not until 1793 that the high wall and lodges were built.

place were a dustbin of incompetence but, fortunately, that is not the case. How could it be, with the hand of Stan Clarke now on the tiller?

Clarke's racing pedigree has involved taking over ailing courses and invigorating them. Chepstow, being in rude health despite ageing and even shabby buildings, presented a different challenge but he has already imposed some of his trademarks – the welcome signs, the racing-green paint and the chattily informative **racecard** – and more will inevitably follow.

The enduring appeal here lies in the setting, the high standard of much of the racing and the established catering and viewing points. Mess with any of this and you risk causing profound offence among notably loyal patrons; many of them were coming here before the original Severn Bridge transformed its accessibility in 1966 and happily tolerate a low-rise stand where the view is limited by pillars.

Much of Chepstow's striking history relates to flat racing. The course was only seven years old when Sir Gordon Richards rode 11 winners at a two-day meeting in 1933, and Lester Piggott registered his comeback winner here after five years of retirement. In feel and appearance, though, this is a jumping track and the St David's Day meeting is one of 13 in the winter season.

If the sun shines on the view over the Wye Valley, Chepstow is heaven, and it needs to be to justify a mid-week member's badge costing £16. For the fare and facilities on offer, this is a price that would be ridiculed anywhere else in the world and Clarke, ever conscious of attracting a younger audience, would be well advised to review it.

The majority, who approach from the English side of the bridge, have paid £4.20 already but the ample signposts are soothing and the **car parks**, once prime territory for tractor rescues from the mud, are now set on gravel. Staff are green-blazered and efficient.

HOW TO GET THERE

By road: On the A446, near to the Severn Bridge.
By rail: To Chepstow; bus service to course.
Admission: Members £16, Tattersalls £11.

Website: www.chepstow-racecourse.co.uk

CATERING

The members' restaurant, a bland room in the basement of the stand, offers no sense of being on a racecourse and demands a revamp. Not so the beloved Persian War Bar, down the slope beyond the winning post and the scene of many a party in the days when racecourse bars did not shut their doors as soon as the last runner passed the post. 'Superior sandwiches' are the speciality and £4.10 is worthwhile for freshly prepared plates of beef, turkey or tuna. The bar offers house wine in quarter-bottles at £3.60 and ample choice of champagne.

At the other end of the course, the Tattersalls Bar keeps mineral

TRACK DETAILS

Chepstow is a left-handed oval nearly 2 miles round. There are 11 fences in a complete circuit.

water and white wine on ice and even provides magazines in racks. Beware on emerging, blinking into the sunshine, for a bet. The ring is huge, but set on a sharp slope, symbolically downhill.

HOTELS, PUBS AND RESTAURANTS

For such a lovely racecourse, options are disappointingly slim. The Marriott, St Pierre Park, is an imposing place to stay and its leisure facilities make it a popular base for weekend racing breaks but you can search in vain for cosier country hotels in the immediate vicinity. Castle View in Bridge Street, which also has a decent bar, probably comes the closest. Further up the Wye

MARKS OUT OF TEN

Access	8
Car parking	8
Comfort and cleanliness	7
Scenery and surroundings	10
Staff attitude	7
Racecard and communication	7
Having a bet	6
Catering	6
Bars	8
Viewing and shelter	4

Total (out of 100) **71**
Ranked joint 23rd out of 59

Hotels, pubs and restaurants
☆☆

Valley there are some enchanting pubs and guest houses and it really is worth the detour if you have the time, but the best of the bunch locally is the Boat, which offers good beer and a split-level restaurant overlooking the river. For eating out in Chepstow, the Wye Knot is a good choice.

- **TOP TIP**: Head up the Wye Valley towards Monmouth.

CHESTER

Marketing men speak of 'the arrival experience', the first impressions that can be so crucial to enjoying an event. Arriving at Chester entails a long queue in a bottleneck of narrow roads before turning in through ancient arches where car repairs and lock-ups evoke more thoughts of Phil Mitchell and Steptoe than Henry Cecil and Shergar.

Thankfully, this is as bad as it gets. The genius of Chester is its impracticality, the absurd notion of shoehorning a racecourse between the natural and unnegotiable borders of city walls and a river. It can never be easy to get in or out but the effort is sublimely worthwhile, even if the cost to pocket and patience can be high.

Of all its beguiling peculiarities, the most startling is the figure of 104,000 who allegedly attended a raceday here in 1946. Even allowing that today's sportsgoer demands more space than his stoical predecessor, this must have involved enough acts of discomfort and contortion to reduce modern health and safety officers to frothing delirium.

Nowadays, the May meeting

The stands at Chester. The large stones in the foreground may have been part of the ancient quay.

53

attracts less than half that number over three days – not counting the hundreds who watch for free from the streets above the walls – but there is no sense of solitude. Indeed, this is one of those rare courses where the intimacy is immediate and addictive. Probably it has been this way since 1511, when the city's Shrovetide fair first included a horse race round the Roodee.

Chester cannot cope comfortably with vast crowds and, despite the best efforts of signposts that divert the unwary miles around the town, the approach roads are stationary two hours before first-race time. There is ample **parking** in centre course, though this is not, as with most tracks, a fallow area.

Such are the confinements here that every square foot has to be profitably employed. Hence the business end of the racing – parade ring, winner's enclosure and weighing-room – are all inside the course, along with a restaurant, a village of

A fine view of the Watergate, through which the horses come, from their Linenhall stables.

private tents and a garden-party atmosphere. All very jolly, especially when the sun shines, for shelter is at a premium.

A novel and effective subway connects with the main stands but, by definition, the sheer fag of a return journey between races deters many from viewing the horses. Their consolation is that the runners are never far away, for this is the smallest circuit in Britain.

Purists, preferring the eye-straining emptiness of the Rowley Mile at Newmarket, sneer at Chester. They call it a 'soup plate' or a 'dog track'. For sure, there are certain types of horse who are best kept away from the place but that does not detract from the compulsive theatre it provides. Watching from the end of the County Stand as the runners hurtle into the short straight is one of the great sights of British racing. It does not, however, come cheap. At Chester, little does. County Stand badges were £30 a day the week I attended, a figure that cannot be justified by the quality of racing, much less by comparison with overseas meetings.

> **TRACK DETAILS**
>
> A left-handed, circular course over 1 mile round with very tight turns. The finishing straight is less than 2 furlongs in distance.

CATERING

The stand is splendid, both in its design for viewing and in its plush and clubby interior. The Long Room, on the first floor, holds a civilised bar, and the County Stand restaurant (lunch £25 a head) could be seen receiving the endorsement of Sir Clement Freud.

It all has an air of exclusivity, firmly protected by a plethora of security staff. Reserved seats, however, incur an extra charge, there is a fee to park cars and the racecard, exemplary in most ways, is £2. If this is all too much, retreat down the course to the Dee Stand, tiny elevated terraces with their original balustrades. It costs £6 and the timeless view is just as good.

HOTELS, PUBS AND RESTAURANTS

There is talk of an August Festival at Chester and it would be a welcome addition to the traditional three days in May.

MARKS OUT OF TEN

Access 5
Car parking 7
Comfort and cleanliness 8
Scenery and surroundings .. 10
Staff attitude 7
Racecard and
communication 8
Having a bet 8
Catering 7
Bars 8
Viewing and shelter 9

Total (out of 100) **77**
Ranked joint 7th out of 59

Hotels, pubs and restaurants
☆☆☆☆

HOW TO GET THERE

By road: The course is accessible from J14 of the M6/M56.
By rail: To Chester General; there is a bus service between the station and the course.
Admission: County Stand £20–£30, Tattersalls £12–£17 (prices vary depending on meeting), Dee Stand £6, course £4.

Website:
www.chester-races.co.uk

This is an atmospheric city, if a shade too lively at night for some tastes, and it is surrounded by a clutch of admirable hotels. Fat wallets will be drawn to the Chester Grosvenor – five stars and prices to match – but less than two miles out of town, the village of Mollington has two fine hotels. Crabwall Manor has the style and the history, Mollington Banastre the modern comforts; both have good restaurants and leisure facilities and there is a village pub attached to the Banastre. Good pubs out of town include the Rising Sun at Tarporley and the Grosvenor Arms at Aldford, which sets a splendid example to all by serving no fewer than 20 wines by the glass. You won't get that at the Albion in Park Street but what you will enjoy is an unspoilt Victorian boozer in a quiet back street with the estimable Timothy Taylors bitter on hand pump.

- **TOP TIP**: Albion pub in Park Street.

DONCASTER

Yorkshire is among my favourite counties. This, I suspect, is worth emphasising now in view of the words to come, for Doncaster boasts none of the assets of the area. The town is an aesthetic eyesore, a culinary vacuum and a sporting backwater and its racecourse, though gallantly improved by vigorous management, cannot quite escape its surroundings.

The shame of this is that the place has such history, such prestige. The course on Town Moor dates back to 1776 and it not only stages

Doncaster's newer stand on the left contrasts with the older buildings.

HOW TO GET THERE

By road: One mile from Doncaster, alongside the M18 (J3 and J4).
By rail: To Doncaster station; bus service runs to course.
Admission: Members £16–£30, grandstand £10–£18, Family Enclosure £4–£6 (prices vary depending on meeting).

Website:
www.britishracing.com

the oldest classic but, by unquestioned right, both opens and closes the turf flat season. However, the Furniture Factors Racing Schools Apprentice Handicap at 1.30 on a March afternoon will not raise much of a fanfare and forgive me if I do not volunteer for the bugle.

Doncaster is a working man's racecourse and there is nothing wrong with that. It is set, after all, in Yorkshire's industrial heartland and it attracts decent, enthusiastic crowds even for a mid-week winter meeting. The fault lies in the assumption that the working class will settle for second best. Just because there is scarcely a restaurant or a pub of note for miles around does not mean the good folk of Doncaster would not like one; the same applies to the browsing and sluicing on their racecourse.

There are some things Doncaster does exceptionally well. It promotes itself energetically and this includes roadsigns, to which some courses remain oddly indifferent. The motorway network decants drivers on to convenient access roads and the one possible delay is at the final roundabout, when the parade of horses from box to stable at least whets the appetite.

Car parks are flat, sensibly surfaced and well marshalled. The air of efficiency continues inside, where an information desk near the main entrance is manned by helpful staff.

Racecards offer the useful quick reference numbering of races and the public address is informative. You will not get lost here, signposts being as plentiful inside the course as on the approach roads, and if the principal purpose of your day is betting, complaints will be few – the ring itself is deep and the betting hall on the ground floor of the stand has ample outlets.

There is a pleasing weighing-room, with elegant stonework and glass dome, but from the stand it is best not to raise the eyes above the horses, even when they disappear from view on the long back straight. The skyline is bleak and industrial; even the floodlights of neighbouring Doncaster Rovers Football Club are redolent of depression.

CATERING

None of this need spoil the day but the impression of dowdiness is maintained inside the cavernous stand. Appointments are either modest or ill-chosen and considering the acreage of tiled floors and gaudy carpets the space is poorly used.

Beneath some of the television screens, hardback chairs are arranged in lines as if it were a doctor's waiting room. Remarkably, people sit there, looking glum and chewing on steak sandwiches from a serving hatch that reminded me of the canteen in my ancient primary school.

A novel but irritating reversible escalator carries racegoers up a level to the Starting Gate cafeteria, which is cheap and not very cheerful. Dry cod and chips, pasty and peas, washed down by instant coffee. Members have a seafood bar, which is dark and dismal, and the second-floor Lincoln Restaurant, where lunch (£18) is served in the type of dining room you would expect in a faded seaside hotel – no view, no atmosphere.

Doncaster makes an effort with families, who have the clean and brightly decorated Silver Patriarch Bar down the

TRACK DETAILS

Left-handed, pear-shaped circuit of 2 miles.

course and even a crèche with baby-changing facilities. But for those who want to eat, drink or simply be merry in civilised surroundings, this is a desert. It is inconceivable that it could be anyone's favourite racecourse.

HOTELS, PUBS AND RESTAURANTS

My bleakest memory of any race meeting recalls a rainy March week when I made the fatal error of booking into one of Doncaster's grim city-centre hotels. The room was dark, the décor faded, the food awful and the town unspeakable. I offer this as a warning to any who may be lulled into doing something similar – avoid it at all costs. Not, it must be added, that there are compelling alternatives close at hand. For pubs, in particular, this is a desert and it must also be one of the worst parts of Britain for decent restaurants. To find a habitable hotel,

---

MARKS OUT OF TEN

Access 6
Car parking 8
Comfort and cleanliness 8
Scenery and surroundings ... 2
Staff attitude 8
Racecard and
communication 6
Having a bet 8
Catering 4
Bars 5
Viewing and shelter 8

Total (out of 100) 63
Ranked joint 46th out of 59

Hotels, pubs and restaurants
☆

---

try Mount Pleasant, close to the course on the A638 at Rossington, or go the extra miles to Blyth, where the Charnwood Hotel is a civilised retreat and the A1 is on the doorstep for a swift getaway.

• **TOP TIP**: Arrive with low expectations.

EPSOM

Among the effects of some frustrated sporting entrepreneur from the dowdy 1950s may possibly lie a design for the perfect racecourse stand in the 21st century. If so, it could bear more than a passing resemblance to the Queen's Stand at Epsom. Stroll through the glass frontage of this imposing white edifice and you are confronted by a blueprint for racegoer satisfaction.

Directly ahead, lavishly produced racecards are sold smilingly from a table; to the right is an information desk and to the left a 'boutique' merchandise stall. Basic needs – so often neglected – are accommodated by a drinking-water dispenser and a taxi freephone. Climb a few steps from the lobby to chic bars and cafés, brightly decorated and fringed by comfortable seating and balconies that overlook the tiny but atmospheric winner's enclosure and the downland course beyond.

It is like being in a capsule, a prototype for aspiring course

Epsom's Prince's stand replaced the 50-year-old original in 1879.

managers. This, you feel, as you take a glass of something chilled from the wine bar on the viewing terrace, is how it should always be. The shame, of course, is that this is not even representative of the rest of Epsom, let alone the rest of the country's racetracks.

Epsom is an energetic place these days. The Derby meeting has been picked off the floor and restored to some of its former glory and there is a gradual regeneration of the minor fixtures, most notably through the racing-and-rock evenings that, here and elsewhere, are claiming a new audience which the sport must continue to cultivate.

Management here is caring and enterprising but, in its shape and structures, the course presents constant problems. Take the **car parks**, for instance: splendidly signposted but set largely on a public golf course, a walk from the entrances. Or take the cheaper alternative to the Queen's Stand, a grandstand that has stood since the First World War and, under close inspection, wears its great age none too well.

On all but one day of Epsom's racing year, it is well worth paying the extra to enjoy the admirable facilities of the Queen's. On Derby day, however, this otherwise democratic place – the people's racecourse by its heritage – comes over all élitist and demands that its Queen's patrons don toppers and tails. Moreover, it imposes the code with stewarding that borders on the officious. It is all so inappropriately pompous, so unnecessary, and it alienates some from a course that otherwise wins high marks for effort and enterprise.

Epsom is only a few miles off the M25 and accessed by a variety of suburban roads. Its signage is good but the trick is to take junction 8, rather than J9, and thus avoid the bottleneck in the town centre.

Pride is taken in the **racecard**. It is doubtless a loss leader, but the impression left by its magazine format is worth the endeavour. Particularly innovative is an index, showing runners and rides for each jockey and trainer present.

Taking the Tattenham Corner at Epsom is one of the high points of the Derby.

CATERING

Catering is generally very good, from the mobile trolleys that offer snacks on the move up to the Blue Riband Restaurant on the Queen's. Little at Epsom comes cheap, though, and lunch is a forbidding £37.50, with wine prices to match. Those who balk at this can eat decent seafood on the same level or head for the first floor of the old stand, where the Café Normandie is sometimes deserted but invariably excellent.

There are plenty of bars, generally bright, inviting and well staffed, but the prices are at the level of London's five-star hotels. Charging £2.50 for a pint of keg bitter is a deterrent – so,

too, £3 for a small glass of wine, or £22 for half a bottle of Moet et Chandon on the Queen's Terrace. Nice place, shame about the rip-off.

HOTELS, PUBS AND RESTAURANTS

Ah, the rolling downs and the stockbroker belt – surely this must be a rich source of food

TRACK DETAILS

Left-handed, U-shaped course, 1.5 miles in extent. The Derby course is uphill for the first half mile, downhill around the final turn and has a half-mile run-in.

MARKS OUT OF TEN

Access 7
Car parking 6
Comfort and cleanliness 7
Scenery and surroundings ... 7
Staff attitude 6
Racecard and
communication 9
Having a bet 8
Catering 8
Bars 7
Viewing and shelter 7

Total (out of 100) 72
Ranked joint 17th out of 59

Hotels, pubs and restaurants
☆

and lodging? Sadly not. The pubs in Epsom tend to the themed, barn-like places beloved of a certain generation but avoided by those who actually recognise the merits of a proper inn. Hotels are either run down or corporate, and restaurants of

note thin on the ground. What on earth must foreigners think of us, to be running the Derby in such a place? There are some civilised pubs – the Sir Douglas Haig and the Plough – in Effingham, the other side of the M25, and nearby Dorking houses the Burford Bridge Hotel. In Cobham, there is a serviceable Hilton and the stylish but expensive Woodlands Park. To eat out, go to Epsom's little sister village, Ewell, and try C'est la Vie.

- TOP TIP: Woodlands Park, if the funds run to it.

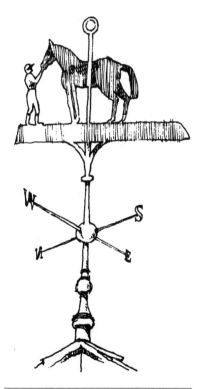

This weathervane representing 'Antler', adorned the Derby stables built in 1854.

HOW TO GET THERE

By road: Well signposted from J8, J9 and J10 of the M25.
By rail: To Epsom, Epsom Downs or Tattenham Corner.
Admission: Queen's Stand £17–£18, grandstand £11–£14. Derby meeting prices are set annually.

Website: www.epsomderby.co.uk

EXETER

There is a touch of masochism about us devotees of jump racing and it was palpable up on Haldon Hill on the day of my visit. All afternoon, teeming rain was whipped into the stands by a malicious wind, yet the faces beamed with contentment. Even when the perennial Exeter fog descended abruptly after the fourth race, a smiling stoicism persisted.

Mad, really, but utterly symptomatic of the jumping mentality when winter approaches. The sport quickens its beat as each downpour cushions the ground, and there are few more authentic settings to witness the changing of the seasons than Exeter.

Only a few years back signs of decline were evident, but the efforts of progressive, communicative management are bearing fruit. The

Caravans mingle with gorse and heather at the Devon and Exeter course at Halden.

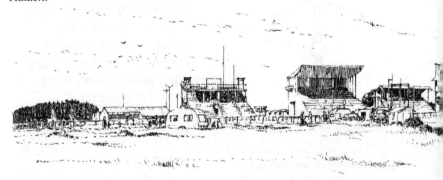

track itself is acknowledged as a classic of the galloping, undulating variety but the paying customers, who once seemed little more than an irritant, are now being included in the deal.

It costs only £11 to watch racing here in a classless society, other than the annual members' bar, and two recent improvements are indicative of a course that has discarded its ill-fitting complacency. The winner's enclosure has been moved from its cramped position in front of the weighing-room and is now a striking feature within the paddock; overlooking both this and the finishing line is an attractive timber deck for disabled racegoers. Too many courses still treat such patrons perfunctorily but Exeter is an honourable exception.

Its position is both ally and enemy. The downside of bordering Dartmoor is the susceptibility to impenetrable fog. The upside is truly enchanting surrounds. Behind and to the west lie some of Britain's finest country hotels and a pub – the Nobody Inn at nearby Doddiscombsleigh – that might just be the best pre-racing detour in the land.

The course lies hard by the A38 dual carriageway, impossible to miss. It is well signposted from the M5, five miles north, and with new yellow directions to the outstanding **car parks** – free, with a hard surface and a dedicated exit road back to the A38.

Small racecourses continue to make financial excuses for poor **racecards** but this too often betrays a laziness in the commercial department. Exeter's is in need of an improvement in design and editorial.

Mitigation comes through a lively public address show that has interviews through the afternoon.

The crowd was treated to Martin Pipe's characteristic pre-race assessment that his runners all had 'no possible chance' and that he 'needed a miracle' to go home with a winner. Naturally, he won the first.

The rush to exploit such 'tips' – or to ignore them – might take Exeter racegoers into the William Hill Bar, where betting and boozing exist side by side in a bright and unthreatening environment that ought to be instructive to those seeking to resist the push for betting in pubs.

CATERING

This is one of two public areas, the Romany King Bar being the other, that combines reasonably priced drinks (wine only £1.50 a glass) with hearty food. I cannot, in honesty, recommend the pasties but the soup tureens and jacket potatoes are ideal for winter. One nitpick – there are not enough seats and too many are occupied by people neither eating nor drinking.

Unusually, the catering is done by the University of Exeter. Staff are young and keen, while the giant signs and menus on every wall give a feel of enterprise. Upstairs in the Desert Orchid Restaurant, lunch is £18.50. There are tables with a view and, though the room is essentially too small, Exeter now displays the foresight to put that right.

TRACK DETAILS

A hilly, right-handed course, galloping in nature. There are 11 fences per circuit, and the half-mile home straight is on the rise all the way to the finish.

HOTELS, PUBS AND RESTAURANTS

On a fine spring day, arrive early, take the exit from the A38 for the course but continue past the driveway towards Dunchideock. Two miles on, turn left and then right for the Nobody Inn at Doddiscombsleigh, quite

HOW TO GET THERE

By road: On the A38, 2 miles east of Chudleigh.
By rail: To Exeter St Davids.
Admission: Grandstand and paddock £12, Silver Ring £5.

Website:
www.exeter-racecourse.co.uk

MARKS OUT OF TEN

Access	9
Car parking	8
Comfort and cleanliness	6
Scenery and surroundings	8
Staff attitude	7
Racecard and communication	7
Having a bet	7
Catering	7
Bars	7
Viewing and shelter	6

Total (out of 100) 72
Ranked joint 17th out of 59

Hotels, pubs and restaurants
☆☆☆☆

possibly the finest pub in Britain. It is everything an inn should be, from the beams, pillars and snug barside benches to the range of ales, excellent bar menu and a wine list that is surely the envy of almost every restaurant in the land. Only its bedrooms are disappointing, but that is hardly a drawback with the variety of overnight options close at hand – even if you do need a good map-reader to find them without getting hopelessly lost on Dartmoor. Haytor is a sweet village with a fine country house hotel, the Bel Alp, and a welcoming pub, the Rock, where the rooms are good. Gidleigh Park at Chagford is only for special treats but the secluded village has other decent hotels. In Exeter itself, St Olave's Court, overlooked by the cathedral, is a nice place to stay and Brazz, an offshoot of the Taunton brasserie, a fun place to eat. The Bridge and the Lighter at Topsham are other pubs for the shortlist in an area rich in choice and quality.

• **TOP TIP:** The Nobody Inn at Doddiscombsleigh.

FAKENHAM

For those familiar with the most closely guarded secret of the English seaside, Fakenham offers guaranteed delight. It is only a few miles from the haven of the north Norfolk coast, so it would scarcely matter if the racecourse was a tip. Thankfully, these days it is rather better than that.

On a spring morning, I can imagine few better agendas than breakfast in Burnham Market, a walk on the deserted expanses of Holkham beach, fresh fish and Adnams for lunch in Brancaster, then a short and self-satisfied drive to the races – not in Fakenham itself but its little sister village, Pudding Norton.

Fakenham is a sleepy, old-fashioned place, as its other splendidly named neighbour, Great Snoring, would suggest. The centre is pedestrianised and the speed limit is a stately 20mph. The horses up the road move faster, though in some cases not by much.

In jump-racing terms, this is an outpost track. The main training centres of Lambourn, Somerset and Yorkshire are all half-a-day's hike

away and, with Newmarket only 50 miles south, it serves a predominantly flat-racing area. It is also a specialists' course, barely a mile round. Interestingly, certain powerful trainers send horses here regularly, lifting an otherwise workaday standard. The balm of jump racing in these surroundings, though, is such that the atmosphere matters far more than the quality.

Approach roads are generally quiet and the signs to the course outstanding. Even the few remaining rail devotees need to drive, the nearest station being 20 miles away, and **car parking**, though mainly on grass, is free and convenient.

Inside, the impression is of a busy, progressive but idiosyncratic venue. The staff are cheerful and alert, though far from intrusive, and the sense that this is a course on the climb is reflected by the building work on a new stand, opened late in 2001. There is also, though, something quirky about the place.

Two signs caught my eye. One, above the door of the first-aid room, announced it to be a 'Vegetable preparation and dishwashing area'. Almost as strange was the ancient edict by the course crossing: 'Please do not walk or jog during frosty weather.' Was this solicitous concern about sprained ankles, overstretching the dishwashing area? I think we should be told.

The parade ring, with its narrow sand track for the horses to plod around, is that of a sophisticated point-to-point. In other ways, though, Fakenham is an example to its alleged betters. Prize money here is good, for instance, and its investment in a full-time physiotherapist for the jockeys' room is admirable.

Bookmakers are sensibly divided between the different

Fakenham racecourse: on the left is the lads' new hostel, and in front of the water-tower the roof of the leisure centre can be seen.

71

enclosures now, a small group clustering in front of a tiny stand down the course. The **racecard** has some individual touches and Derek Thompson's intimate tones usually boom from the public address. You can't have everything.

> **TRACK DETAILS**
>
> Left-handed, undulating, tight track of 1 mile, with six fences to a circuit and a 250-yard run-in.

Spectator facilities are limited but there is no feel of depression. The ancient main stand, with uninterrupted viewing, has creeper on its rear as a kind of anti-ageing cosmetic and even an intensely ugly building down the course is somehow made to work as a base for brunches and a viewing point of the home turn. It would, though, be a prettier course for its demolition.

CATERING

A large marquee provides shelter, provisions and unexpected style. There is a raised matting floor, heaters around the walls and chandeliers overhead. Home-made lunches and good coffee are served at one end, drinks in the centre and a hog roast – one of three on the course – near the entrance. If this is a temporary amenity, it has been created with care.

There are rustic hot chestnut and cheese stalls and a coffee bar on a wooden terrace, which would be much better if they served proper coffee. The main bar is spartan, with bare boards on the floor. No complaints, though, about the tiny real ale tent, with Adnams from the barrel. Cause, perhaps, for another night in Burnham Market?

HOTELS, PUBS AND RESTAURANTS

North Norfolk is one of the most civilised and relaxing areas in Britain for a short break and Fakenham is conveniently central.

HOW TO GET THERE

By road: The track is 21 miles east of Kings Lynn and 26 miles west of Norwich, on the A419 and A148.
By rail: Liverpool Street to Norwich, then taxi to course.
Admission: Members £15, grandstand and paddock £10, course £5.

Website: www.fakenhamrace-course.co.uk

MARKS OUT OF TEN

Access 8
Car parking 6
Comfort and cleanliness 7
Scenery and surroundings ... 8
Staff attitude 7
Racecard and communication 6
Having a bet 8
Catering 7
Bars 5
Viewing and shelter 7

Total (out of 100) 69
Ranked joint 33rd out of 59

Hotels, pubs and restaurants
☆☆☆☆☆

Just outside the town, the Old Rectory at Great Snoring is a charming small hotel, but within 20 minutes' drive you can be at any of three seriously good bases. Morston Hall, just outside Blakeney on the coast road, has six spacious rooms and a top-class restaurant; Congham Hall at Grimston is bigger but far from impersonal; and the Hoste Arms at Burnham Market is a modern wonder, mixing pub, hotel and brasserie food without sacrificing quality. Yetman's at Holt is another good restaurant but this area is at its best in the supply of country pubs – some absurdly undiscovered – with good beer (Adnams and Woodfordes) and excellent food. The Red Lion at Stiffkey, the Three Horseshoes at Warham All Saints and the Jolly Fisherman at Brancaster are three personal favourites but then I could go on...

• **TOP TIP**: Hoste Arms at Burnham Market.

73

FOLKESTONE

Approaching Folkestone racecourse on a colourless January day is a little like driving on to the set of an old film. *The Land That Time Forgot*, perhaps. A derelict, Hitchcockian motel spoils the view from the A20 and the single, narrow access road winds on to the type of quaint railway station that the Beeching plan tried to abolish.

Cars are parked haphazardly in a series of small fields – boots advisable – and the first thing to take the eye once inside is a quintessentially Kentish stand in white weatherboard, its paint fading with its former glory. Other strange buildings resemble conservatories or garden sheds and the leafless trees in the parade ring, attractive in summer, are as stark now as the condemned terracing further down the course. Oh dear.

The only racecourse in Kent has survived some perilous times of late, and perhaps its extinction would not be widely mourned. It has been added to

Westenhanger House at Folkestone racecourse gives a dimension of history few other courses have.

the portfolio of the acquisitive Arena group, now diversifying from all-weather tracks and intent on increasing its percentage of the fixture list with the end game of global Internet pictures. This incentive, sharply identified and singlemindedly pursued, does not, in itself, guarantee the future of the course, which remains in considerable doubt.

Arena has been in residence for two years and the improvements are so far superficial – red-and-white branding on racecards and signs, for instance. Longer-term ambitions are much grander.

A new access road is planned, along with a centre-course car park, hopefully more shoe-friendly. Arena loves hotels and will apply to build one here; there will also be a new stable block and, best of all, the original stand will be restored and refurbished.

Unless all of this passes the drawing-board stage, Folkestone must be judged for what it is, which is run down. This is a part of Kent that must now forever be tunnel territory and it is bland beyond redemption, an image the course does nothing to correct. Passengers on Eurostar can actually view racing as their trains slow for the descent to France; what they see will not make many wish to disembark early.

It may seem a long way from almost anywhere but it has in its favour proximity to the M20 and raceday trains from Charing Cross. There are no class barriers here – the £12 admission allows you to roam anywhere you please. Cars are parked free and the green-blazered Arena staff are plentiful and efficient.

The **racecard** is clear and colourful, with a readable form guide and some enterprising offers for the string of midwinter jumping

Weatherboarding and an ornamental pond at Folkestone's course.

meetings, mostly transferred here from Lingfield. Gather ten friends for the day and you can have a private box with a three-course lunch, and even name a race, for £42.95 a head. Initiatives like that, in an outlet often insultingly over-priced, deserve to drag in a few extra punters – and Folkestone needs every one it can get.

CATERING

New caterers are feeling their way. You can lunch with a view in the Lookout Restaurant for £21 or eat ham, egg and chips

TRACK DETAILS

The course is right-handed, about 11 furlongs round, with easy turns. There are seven fences to a circuit, with a 1 furlong run-in.

for £3 in the ramshackle Paddock Café at the rear of the old stand. Avoid at all costs the Glover Bar, which not only has the depressing air of a 1950s' station buffet but serves packet sandwiches and instant coffee to reinforce the image.

The betting area is small but easily viewed from open terracing behind. There are few places to watch the racing under cover, so retreat to the old stand, which not only offers a decent view but the treat of the course, in a bar with the bare boards, armchairs and ambience of a slightly faded gentleman's club. Drink acceptable house wine in 25cl bottles at £3.60 and think back to 1898 when the course was new and, doubtless, considered rather swanky. How times change.

HOTELS, PUBS AND RESTAURANTS

It is hard to think of a good reason to go to Folkestone other than as a launch pad for leaving the country. The area has a neglected feel, borne out by the shortage of good dining and lodging, and Kent's reputation for good pubs does not extend this far south. The Clifton, up high on the Leas with views out to sea, calls itself 'Folkestone's premier hotel' but this is to claim faint praise indeed. Nearby Sandgate, on the Hythe side of the town, saves the day with the estimable Sandgate Hotel but even here there is a significant catch. The hotel's fine

MARKS OUT OF TEN	
Access	7
Car parking	4
Comfort and cleanliness	5
Scenery and surroundings	3
Staff attitude	7
Racecard and communication	5
Having a bet	6
Catering	6
Bars	7
Viewing and shelter	5
Total (out of 100)	**55**

Ranked 57th out of 59

Hotels, pubs and restaurants ☆

restaurant, La Terrasse, is closed on Monday and Tuesday lunchtimes, which is pretty inconvenient for visitors to a course that stages most of its racing on those days. Try the Clarendon pub, also in Sandgate, for decent food and plenty of wines.

• **TOP TIP**: Sandgate Hotel.

77

FONTWELL

Americans would not understand Fontwell Park. They simply wouldn't see the point of it. Nor, come to that, would Australians or Asians or many of our European neighbours because, when it comes down to it, most of the world is boring and uniform where racecourses are concerned and can only be pitied for what they are missing.

Fontwell is probably the best small racecourse in the south but try explaining its merits to a native New Yorker, reared on stereotyped,

The old village post office on the left became a hostel for the stable-girls.

sliderule-flat, left-handed tracks where everything is just so, and prepare to watch eyes glaze over.

Here, in affluent West Sussex, lies a hilly hurdle track just a mile round and, inside it, a figure-of-eight chase course with dizzying cambers and corners. There are five grandstands, most of which could comfortably be filled by a coachload of corpulent Californians.

Behind them a patchwork of cosy country buildings gives way startlingly to a manicured garden with Grecian ornaments, a pagoda and a classical country house. Come to think of it, the Americans would love that bit – and if Fontwell made more of the fact that the Queen owned her first winner here, 51 years ago, there might even be a market for those coach parties.

Fontwell, though, is doing fine. Crowds are up and deservedly so, for the facilities are almost unrecognisable from a decade ago and the progress has been made without sacrificing an atmosphere warmer than on any other track in this most reserved part of the country.

It could hardly be easier to find Fontwell, for it borders the A27 trunk road at the point where signs subject drivers to the abnormal command: 'No racing by horse-drawn vehicles.' Apparently this is unconnected to proceedings inside, where, once beyond the pitted and puddled **car park** (improvements needed), the friendliness is instantly evident.

The **racecard**, price £1.50, has a colour cover and an innovative pictorial guide to facilities. Giant maps are also posted on the grandstand walls and there is a quaint shop and information desk. Such signs of striving to impress continue among the essentials – the loos, that great barometer of care, are immaculate.

This is a lovely part of Sussex and the course, secluded by trees, feels suitably rural despite its proximity to the main south coast road. The paddock has viewing terraces at three points but the winner's enclosure, outside the bland bungalow of a weighing-room, is a disappointment.

79

CATERING

For a drink, head first to the democratic Salmon Spray Bar, between the paddock and the stands. Here, Gales bitter tapped from the barrel was selling at £1.50 a pint. Each of the varied bars is well stocked, staffed and furnished, to a point where some plainly find it hard to drag themselves out for the racing.

The same is true of the lunchers in Fontwell House, so elegant that it is no surprise it has another life as a wedding venue. A three-course meal here is £25 and the setting is soothing, if somewhat detached from the business of the day.

Closer to the action, two of the main bars have seafood dining areas and a third sells a variety of curries at £4 a time. For style on the run, the Lawn Bar offers good coffee and freshly made baps so vast and well filled that it is hard to finish one between races. Half-bottles of champagne are another good touch here.

The betting ring is set hard against the Tattersalls stand and is usually lively, but to capture

the essence of Fontwell, leave the eating, drinking and punting for an hour, don stout shoes and proceed to centre course for one of the true spectacles of National Hunt.

Near the intersection of the figure of eight, you can join a sizeable, devoted group that shuttles between a downhill fence, hairy for horse and rider, and the last up the wearying hill. In marathon races, such as the

MARKS OUT OF TEN	
Access	8
Car parking	5
Comfort and cleanliness	8
Scenery and surroundings	8
Staff attitude	7
Racecard and communication	7
Having a bet	7
Catering	9
Bars	9
Viewing and shelter	8

Total (out of 100) 76
Ranked joint 9th out of 59

Hotels, pubs and restaurants
☆☆☆

HOW TO GET THERE

By road: Between Arundel and Chichester, close to the junction of the A27 and A29.
By rail: From Victoria or London Bridge to Barnham, then taxi or free coach to course.
Admission: Members £15, Tattersalls £10, Silver Ring £6.

Website: www.fontwellpark.co.uk

TRACK DETAILS

The chase course is a figure of eight, while the hurdles track is a left-handed oval about 1 mile round.

televised Sussex National, the process is repeated three times, and few go home disappointed. I think, though, they should erect a sign on the course crossing – 'No coach parties' – just in case.

HOTELS, PUBS AND RESTAURANTS

Though set alongside the hectic south coast trunk road, Fontwell contrives a rural feel, borne out by a treasure-chest of country pubs amid the nearby South Downs. The Black Horse at Byworth lies north-east, the Fox Goes Free at Singleton north-west, and both are rewarding detours from the main roads. Closer to the course, the Murrell Arms at Barnham and the Holly Tree at Walberton attract plenty of pre-race business and the Woodmans Arms at Hammerpot, towards Worthing on the A27, is a good stopping point after the last. Hotels in this area cater for all tastes, from the opulence of Bailiffscourt at Climping downwards. Many have a corporate bias but to avoid this, try the restful Findon Manor, just north of Worthing, where the rooms are spacious, the food good and the bonus is watching Josh Gifford's string at work on the Downs before breakfast.

• **TOP TIP:** Findon Manor Hotel.

81

GOODWOOD

There is something about Goodwood that does not merely evoke thoughts of shimmering summer days, it positively demands them. More than any other premier league racecourse, this jewel amid the Sussex downs depends on sunshine for its sparkle. On the basis that a place is best judged in adversity, then, the sea fret and driving rain of a repellent May day were ideal.

Glorious it was not. But neither was it forlorn, much less forbidding. The rudest remarks about Goodwood, down the years, have

concerned its snobbery, from the haughtiness of the staff to the formality of presentation. Thankfully, as at Ascot, attitudes have softened and the product has benefited for it.

Until the 1960s, Goodwood staged only four days' racing each year. Commercial reality had no meaning here. Now it is part of the diverse leisure and tourist industry around this charming Sussex village, featuring on plentiful signs on the variety of approach roads alongside the motor circuit, the museum and the golf course.

It is not cheap to go racing here, but at a maximum £18 for all days other than Glorious Goodwood it is not outlandish, either. Encouraging youth, the age limit on free entry is 17 here, rather than the usual 16. **Car parks** are exemplary, though not all are free.

Litter is cleared rapidly and the loos, that great gauge of efficiency, are kept pristine. Goodwood still has its standards – 'jeans, bare midriffs and hot pants are not permitted' in the Richmond enclosure

A view looking towards Trundle Hill, shows the Richmond stand with its distinctive roof supports.

Elisabeth Frink's horse by Goodwood's Richmond stand leads the eye beyond to Chichester.

– but there is now a gratifying air of staging a show rather than defending a museum. It will impress even more when the present inadequate parade ring is replaced.

The **racecard** meets the strictest criteria of layout, information, editorial and – even at £2 – value. There is a merchandise shop, ideal for anyone seeking a pair of gaudy yellow-and-red braces, but far more customer-friendly is the constantly updated noticeboard, with news and reactions from the day's racing, and the initiative of mini-buses taking adventurous spectators down to the start.

Goodwood has even adopted a recent chart hit as its theme music. This may have a few dukes and lords, dead and alive, seething incandescently, for the cast list here would grace a P. G. Wodehouse novel. The third Duke of Richmond staged the first meeting, 199 years ago, for the pleasure of his army chums, but it was the formidable Lord George Bentinck who established

HOW TO GET THERE

By road: The course is 4 miles north of Chichester, and can be reached via the A27, A286 or A285.
By rail: To Chichester; a bus service operates between the station and the course on race-days.
Admission: Richmond enclosure £19, Gordon enclosure £12, public enclosure £5; Festival meeting (August): Richmond is members only, Gordon enclosure £20, public enclosure £8.

Website: www.goodwood.co.uk

TRACK DETAILS

The pronounced downhill gradients from the home turn make this a sharp track. The 5-furlong course is one of the fastest in the country.

Goodwood as a pioneer. As manager in the 1820s, he was the first to introduce paddock parades and number cloths.

CATERING

Bentinck is commemorated by a bar in the March Stand that epitomises the high standards of what Wodehouse would have called 'the browsing and sluicing'. The drink is costly – £4 for a quarter-bottle of wine is prohibitive – but the bars are slickly staffed and sensibly designed, with railings to encourage orderly queues.

Food is imaginative, from the chicken jalfrezi and braised rib-eye available in both the Richmond and cheaper Gordon enclosures to the Front Runner burger bar and pizza outlet. Best of all, at least when the sun shines, is the alfresco seafood dining on the Richmond lawn, as agreeable a racing lunch as can be had in all of Britain.

Gawp at the wondrous views across the downs, observe the uniquely shaped course from stands designed to please as well as shelter, then pick a post-race pub from the delightful selection nearby. Bliss. Even when it rains.

HOTELS, PUBS AND RESTAURANTS

For the July meeting many hotels cash in with all-inclusive packages that demand a large outlay, a minimum of three nights stay and dining in. The best places are booked up months in advance. At other times, the choice is good and the pace more leisurely. Nowhere could be more convenient than the Marriott, Goodwood Park and the facilities, including a leisure club and pool, are unarguably high class. Towards the sea, the villages of Bosham and Emsworth are worth exploring – the former boasts the Millstream Hotel and the latter two good restaurants in Spencers and 36 On The Quay. Personal choice takes me back to Midhurst, 15 minutes north of the course, where the Angel and the Spread Eagle share the

MARKS OUT OF TEN	
Access	8
Car parking	7
Comfort and cleanliness	8
Scenery and surroundings	10
Staff attitude	8
Racecard and communication	8
Having a bet	7
Catering	8
Bars	7
Viewing and shelter	9
Total (out of 100)	**80**

Ranked joint 3rd out of 59

Hotels, pubs and restaurants
☆☆☆☆☆

same ownership but offer characterful hotels of individual distinction. The Angel, where front-facing rooms can suffer from traffic noise, also has an outstanding brasserie. Welcoming pubs adorn the area, with the Fox Goes Free at Singleton and the White Horse at Chilgrove both exceptional.

● **TOP TIP**: Angel at Midhurst.

HAMILTON

The winning post at Hamilton Park is draped in roses. On another course, this might be no more than tokenism, a spot of window dressing on a gloomy, grimy shop, but here it is indicative of the full production. Everything at Hamilton is neat and much of it is stylish, which comes as a considerable surprise once the precarious history of the place is known.

Hamilton has lived dangerously. Created in 1888 by request of local whisky magnates, it was closed for 20 years either side of the First World War by a duchess who disapproved of gambling, and as recently as the 1970s suffered such a parlous period that permanent closure threatened.

Between times, Hamilton pioneered evening racing and morning racing, a runaway success and a transient misjudgement. Life, here, has plainly never been dull and seldom secure but there is now such a tangible vibrancy that it is hard to see why the future should be jeopardised again.

This is one of those apparently isolated tracks that draw raised eyebrows and snorts of cynicism from the southern majority who regard a trip to York as the annual voyage of discovery. It is not, though, hard to find. Keep going up the M6, on to the M74, and there it is at junction 5, attentively signposted.

Cross the River Clyde and enter one of the well-surfaced **car parks**, tidily organised by the first of an army of staff in smart designer jackets. This series has made much of 'the welcome experience', those all-important first impressions, and Hamilton does it better than most. Racegoers are made to feel immediately important, which

Looking up the straight to the brown and white grandstand. To the right the ground falls steeply to the Clyde valley.

should put them in the mood to appreciate the manicured lawns, plentiful benches, fresh paint and original music. It was Independence Day when I visited, hence a pre-race diet of American classics.

The **racecard** is a let-down and requires some imaginative input. The winner's enclosure is too small, if we are nitpicking, and the jockeys would doubtless say the same about the weighing-room, though this miniature country cottage with pillars and hanging baskets must be preserved, whatever the needs of modernity.

CATERING

These, anyway, have already been well serviced by an outstanding conversion of the main stand that is, in most ways, a model for small courses to imitate. From the outside it looks chic, with plentiful glass and white paint. Inside, there is a viewing restaurant that might be a fashionable London eatery, along with a café and bar.

Experience, however, did not match appearance. At the Panoramic Café, I waited five minutes at an unattended counter only to be told that their stock of snacks was down to one soggy tuna roll – and this after only two races. My complaint did bring action and a promise that 'the chef will make something fresh', but the maxim must be that attractive areas only fulfil a purpose if they are properly stocked.

No such problems in the bars. The Dukes Room, with its clear glass frontage allowing a view of the racing for plenty of drinkers, is as spectacular as Joe Punters, at the rear of the stand next to the betting hall, is whimsical. Both whisky and wine were a reasonable £1.90 per glass. In Cats, the champagne bar, there is a choice of two bubblies by the glass, something else other courses could profitably copy.

Those punters who venture into the ring are rewarded by a neatly railed area down a flight of steps from the grandstand terrace, a novel design that avoids crush. Detailed thought

HOW TO GET THERE

By road: The course is on the B7071 Bothwell Road, Hamilton, and can be reached from J5 of the M74.
By rail: To Hamilton West, which is near the course.
Admission: Club £12–£15 (prices vary depending on meeting), public enclosure £8.

Website: www.hamilton-park.co.uk

has also gone into such facilities as the toilets – all new and plentiful – and the extension of the stand roof to provide proper shelter.

Hamilton has not yet got everything right – the restaurant, for instance, became uncomfortably hot – but there is a sense that mistakes and deficiencies will rapidly be addressed. It is an unexpectedly pretty course, thick trees forming a shield from the motorway, and if the racing is of uniformly modest standard, the same cannot be said for the enjoyment factor.

TRACK DETAILS

A mile and 5 furlongs in extent, with a run-in of 5 furlongs. Undulating for the most part, with a severe hill to climb at the finish.

MARKS OUT OF TEN

Access	8
Car parking	7
Comfort and cleanliness	8
Scenery and surroundings	6
Staff attitude	8
Racecard and communication	5
Having a bet	9
Catering	5
Bars	8
Viewing and shelter	8

Total (out of 100) 73
Ranked 16th out of 59

Hotels, pubs and restaurants
☆

HOTELS, PUBS AND RESTAURANTS

It is enough of a surprise to find such a trim, immaculate racecourse in this largely unprepossessing area off the M74. It would have been truly remarkable to find it dotted with agreeable hostelries. A good job, then, that Glasgow is only ten miles distant. The Bothwell Bridge, a three-star hotel, stands out as an oasis close to the course but good pubs and restaurants are in distinctly short supply. The style and substance of modern Glasgow makes up for a lot, though, and Malmaison and One Devonshire Gardens are just two among many admirable places to stay. Restaurants abound in the city and a fun pub worth a visit is the Babbity Bowster in Blackfriars Street.

• **TOP TIP**: Don't waste time, head for Glasgow.

HAYDOCK

Many racecourses would shrink from staging a meeting on Derby day, but someone has to do it and Haydock Park is one of few that can be thought up to the challenge. The racing may suffer by comparison with events at Epsom but the show will be slick and the customer satisfaction high.

Among the 18 tracks that put on both flat and National Hunt, Haydock is a market leader. There will be southern courses that demur but here, more than anywhere, is a sense that the two codes share equal billing. At Ascot, the jumping comes across as an afterthought. Sandown would be better off concentrating on National Hunt and leaving flat racing to its sister track, Kempton. Newbury makes a decent fist of both but Haydock has the edge.

The plaudits must begin on the M6, where tourist

A mixture of old and new at Haydock.

Haydock still has older stands to give a touch of past styles.

signs siphon race traffic off at junction 23, from where the course is clearly visible. There is an ordered access system and the **car parks** – free, well stewarded and mostly tarmaced – are among the best in the country.

A smart reception area gives an air of style and occasion, the staff smile on cue and, inside, all is trim and manicured. There are helpful signposts for newcomers and timber benches under the tall trees round the parade ring that might almost belong to a country park.

Hard to believe this is the industrial north-west. Even from the stands, which contain an unusual number of seats with an intimate view of the finishing post, the outlook is inoffensive, ample trees acting as a blind to the churning motorway beyond. It is not the prettiest outlook in racing but not the ugliest, either.

The **racecard** is glossy, clear and colourful and would benefit only from a few articles to justify its £2 price tag. Among the best of Haydock's innovations is a closed-circuit television show for its weekend meetings, including race previews and interviews. This is the standard of audience entertainment, regulation in the USA, that will be increasingly demanded by a new generation of British racegoers. Haydock is ahead of the game, though has some catching up to do regarding its inadequate winner's enclosure, soon to be moved and expanded.

It is on Saturdays that Haydock really comes alive, with crowds of above 10,000, but it is also here that their problems begin. Proximity to Manchester and Liverpool is such that this is a favourite venue for lads' days out, and when the intake of ale and

> ## TRACK DETAILS
>
> A left-handed, oval-shaped course that is galloping in nature.

volume of voices are at their peak, some of the bars become unappealing. Haydock has decent security but the beery brawl at a recent meeting was not an isolated incident. This is a shame, for the place has so much to commend it.

CATERING

The bars are cheap, with bitter at £2 a pint and glasses of drinkable wine at £2.10, but they are also attractive, carpeted and spacious. The champagne bar is a civilised spot but for those who really want to trade up, Haydock offers a Premier area at £35 a head. On the face of it this is an outrageous price, but there has been no shortage of takers, either at the basic charge or the £60 per person that includes a meal in Harry's Bistro, which might easily be your neighbourhood wine bar. A balcony offers the best view of racing and the enterprise of Haydock in pro-

viding such an élite, clubby area is to be applauded.

For one-tenth of the price, the Newton, Haydock's superior Silver Ring, is good enough for many. Here you will find a children's playground, picnic areas and a cosy, family feel. Overall, this is a pleasingly democratic course, where people find their level without feeling awkward.

HOTELS, PUBS AND RESTAURANTS

The sprawling industrial areas of Lancashire do not lend themselves to leisure and pleasure, so a fine

93

HOW TO GET THERE

By road: Via the M6 (J23) and then the A49.
By rail: To Newton le Willows, then taxi to course; a bus service runs from Wigan station.
Admission: Premier £30–£35, County Stand £17–£21,Tattersalls £10–£13, Newton £5–£6.

Website:
www.haydock-park.com and www.haydock-park.co.uk

MARKS OUT OF TEN

Access 10
Car parking 9
Comfort and cleanliness 9
Scenery and surroundings ... 5
Staff attitude 8
Racecard and communication 8
Having a bet 7
Catering 8
Bars 7
Viewing and shelter 8

Total (out of 100) **79**
Ranked 5th out of 59

Hotels, pubs and restaurants
☆

racecourse is inevitably deficient in this regard. It is a barren land for congenial pubs but what Haydock does have is serviceable hotels on the doorstep, with the Thistle and Post House both within walking distance of the gates. They are safe, comfortable but predictably sterile. Just off the M62 in Warrington lie two more huge and well-appointed hotels, the Park Royal and Daresbury Park, each with exemplary leisure facilities. Decent dining in this area is pretty much confined to the hotels unless you make the detour into Manchester, where Simply Heathcote's, a city-centre brasserie, and Yang Sing, possibly the best Chinese eaterie in England, make the journey worthwhile.

• **TOP TIP**: Detour to Manchester for food and lodging.

HEREFORD

Alongside the road to Hereford stands an interesting variation on a racecourse sign. 'Danger', it says. 'Hop Picking Tractors.' This is the kind of bucolic seduction expected from these parts and the image persists over the hills, past orchards, through such pretty hamlets as Ocle Pychard and into a course that, sadly, banishes romanticism at a glance.

There is nothing of the rural idyll about Hereford. The view takes in a functional leisure centre, hockey and cricket pitches, gasworks, car dealerships and a newspaper plant. At least the cider factory is nicely symbolic of the county, but the picture as a whole is dismayingly prosaic.

Perhaps it is best summed up by Peter Scudamore, whose family is so steeped in the place that his late grandfather, Geoffrey, recalled riding around the course three different ways. 'It is a town course in the country', he said, which may explain the pervasive sense of an identity crisis.

Having recently been taken over by Stan Clarke's expanding empire, soon it will receive the green-paint-and-band-music treatment and, on past evidence, it may emerge flourishing, with a smarter facade, better signs and car parks and a **racecard** conveying something more of the place than mere runners and riders.

Certainly, Hereford requires investment but it also requires more enterprise than its present council ownership promotes. The catchment area is small but the patronage is loyal, chiefly from the farming community. The atmosphere is genial, the accents rustic, the complexions ruddy. The racing is low grade but often, it seems to me, eventful.

Some years ago, on a baking bank holiday, a slow, staying chaser in which I owned a leg was 25 lengths clear of a field of plodders. Turning into the Hereford straight, one fence to jump and years of frustration about to be redeemed, his saddle slipped and the jockey fell off.

Now it could be that this incident coloured my judgement of Hereford for ever and yet my last visit began with a nine-runner novices' hurdle in which the leader fell at the last and brought down the next two, leaving a pair of stragglers to fight out a slow-motion finish. Things do seem to happen here.

Hereford has always seemed a maze – one wrong turn and you are heading back to Worcester. More signs would be welcome, along with stricter supervision of a **car park** that is often chaotic by late afternoon.

The course forms a 12-furlong square, so the back straight seems pretty distant, but the view from the low-rise stands is uninterrupted. As the ground rises from the track, the lawns and benches are good

Hereford has a glorious vista of the city and the hills. Here the cider factory contrasts with the cathedral.

vantage points, too, but this is not a place where the view will detain you when the race is over.

There is the feel of a point-to-point about the rudimentary paddock, while the winner's enclosure is tucked apologetically into a corner. There is no ceremony here, no show at all really.

CATERING

Inside, things improve markedly. The bars are carpeted and civilised, with picture windows lending a sense of air and involvement. Lager is overpriced at £2.40 a pint but the local cider is popular at £2.20 and there is mulled wine on tap in winter. House champagne and quarter-bottles of wine are reasonable.

Other than the surrounding countryside, such a contrast to the course itself, the best feature of Hereford is its food. Some will aver that nothing can beat prawn curry from the seafood hut by the paddock but the dining area in the clubhouse is excellent.

Tables, some with a view of racing, can be reserved for £5 a head. A hearty carvery lunch costs £10.95 and the puddings are mouthwatering. The coffee is palatable, which cannot be said for the Tattersalls buffet, which also labours under the misapprehension that modern farmers are made of money by charging an exorbitant £2.20 for sausage rolls or pasties.

HOTELS, PUBS AND RESTAURANTS

If the course itself seems criminally misplaced in an area as close to urban as Hereford can get, the surroundings

TRACK DETAILS

Right-handed square track of 1 mile 4 furlongs, with nine fences to a circuit and a 300-yard run-in.

HOW TO GET THERE

By road: Via A40 and A49 from the south, or M5, M50 and A49 from the north.
By rail: To Hereford station, then 1 mile by taxi.
Admission: Club £15, Tattersalls £10, Silver Ring £5.

Website: www.hereford-racecourse.co.uk

MARKS OUT OF TEN

Access 6
Car parking 5
Comfort and cleanliness 7
Scenery and surroundings ... 6
Staff attitude 6
Racecard and communication 3
Having a bet 6
Catering 7
Bars 7
Viewing and shelter 8

Total (out of 100) **61**
Ranked 52nd out of 59

Hotels, pubs and restaurants
☆☆☆☆

compensate fully. This is a beguiling county where to drive for 20 minutes in any direction is to encounter at least a couple of beckoning pubs and a pleasant country hotel. Hereford itself is not badly served, either, with the reputation of the Castle House Hotel, alongside the river and 100 yards from the cathedral, steeply enhanced by the AA award of national hotel of the year. Castle House also has a terrific restaurant, but for those who seek something of a pubbier feel, take the A465 out of town to Ruckhall where the Ancient Camp, named after a Stone Age fort, offers Hook Norton ale and fine food. Towards Ross-on-Wye, the Lough Pool at Sellack has a peaceful setting and charming atmosphere, while the village of Woolhope has two good pubs, the Butchers Arms and the Crown. The Crown and Anchor at Lugwardine is even closer to the course.

• **TOP TIP**: Ancient Camp at Ruckhall.

HEXHAM

By sustaining such a volume and diversity of courses, many of them economically and geographically challenged, British racing polarises its supporters. Many, thankfully, believe that this unrivalled variety is the essential appeal of the sport but some contend hotly that it would be a more affluent, impressive and manageable industry if what they consider the rustic irrelevances were banished.

Those holding this extreme view might start their cull with Hexham. Their case may focus on the primitive facilities, the generally dire standard of racing, the average crowds of barely 2,000. No doubt they could go on, citing the exposure to the worst of weather that accounts for an uncomfortable number of fixtures.

Even the defence that Hexham, in its isolated setting just the right side of Hadrian's Wall, offers racing to an otherwise starved area is no longer strictly true. The local newspaper fears the place is becoming 'a ghost town' as everyone heads 20 miles east to Newcastle for shopping and leisure. Perhaps racing, too?

It is not easy to make a convincing argument for racing at Hexham unless you have been there on a sunlit evening in early summer, taking the stunning road across the north Pennines to the quaint town with its seventh-century abbey, then climbing two miles to the vertiginous course at Yarridge Heights. So long as the wind is gentle, the setting is such that most things can be forgiven.

Hexham is the heartland of rural racing and that, in some traditional minds, is sufficient cause to celebrate and protect it. The suspicion, however, that younger generations will need rather more persuasion means that this course, and its like, cannot exist complacently in the past.

Money is one drawback to modernisation, aesthetic sensitivity another. No point in having a scenic jewel such as this and ruining it with red brick. There are things that can be done, though, to improve some of the most basic facilities in the country, and the Ramshaw Stand, completed only two years ago, could and should have achieved most of the priorities. Instead, bafflingly, it is not really a stand at all, for there is no terracing and no outside seats. It resembles a cheaply built three-storey hotel on the ring road of a commuter town and represents a lost opportunity.

At a less ambitious level, they could start by placing more signposts to the racing, steward the **car parks** more efficiently and improve the ramshackle entrance gates. On the plus side, club admission is a realistic £10 and the **racecard** is at least bright, clear and only £1.

The view from the parade ring at Hexham illustrates the isolation of the course.

This is a country track for country people and needs to be judged as such, but the wooden shed with its corrugated iron roof that offers a rudimentary shelter alongside the parade ring is an eyesore.

CATERING

Catering outlets are limited. Upstairs in the Ramshaw there is a beef and pork carvery, while the Bramble Tudor Bar above the paddock has fresh rolls

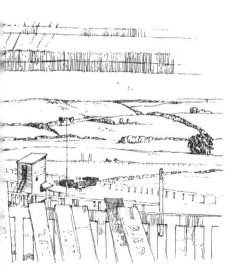

along with its staple diet of pie and peas. The Pavilion Restaurant is like a jaunty seaside tearoom but the Shire Bar – canned beer, screw-top wine, instant coffee and musty atmosphere – is in urgent need of attention.

Nobody should go to Hexham to feel pampered and well fed. It is a rural idyll where one can stand on steps and lawns for a panoramic view of racing that hardly rises above the quality of point-to-point. Thankfully, some of it is now staged in summer.

HOTELS, PUBS AND RESTAURANTS

Standing on the windswept heights of this racecourse,

HOW TO GET THERE

By road: The course is 1.5 miles south-west of Hexham, reached via the A69.
By rail: Hexham station, then a short taxi ride.
Admission: Members £12, Tattersalls £8.

Website: www.hexham-racecourse.co.uk

MARKS OUT OF TEN

Access 4
Car parking 5
Comfort and cleanliness 5
Scenery and surroundings .. 10
Staff attitude 6
Racecard and
communication 5
Having a bet 7
Catering 5
Bars 6
Viewing and shelter 7

Total (out of 100) 60
Ranked joint 53rd out of 59

Hotels, pubs and restaurants
☆☆☆

Hexham can feel many miles from civilisation. In fact, its proximity to Hadrian's Wall makes it something of a tourist mecca and there are numerous cosy guest houses in the pleasant town centre and surrounding villages. The Hexham Royal Hotel is reliable and convenient but perhaps the most stylish place to stay is Langley Castle, a 14th-century castle with luxurious rooms, several sporting four-poster beds. Out of town, Slaley Hall Hotel has good rooms, a leisure club and a championship golf course in a relaxing setting. Agreeable pubs are plentiful, with Dipton Mill and the Rose and Crown in Hexham itself and the Milecastle Inn, serving Jennings beer in historic Haltwhistle, all good choices.

• TOP TIP: Slaley Hall Hotel.

HUNTINGDON

Some of us grow romantically attached to our racecourses, anticipating the next visit like a lustful date. Huntingdon, plain and uninspiring to the eye, will never be a course to make the heart sing but a day in the flatlands of Cambridgeshire need no longer be regarded as a social chore.

Words such as 'unpretentious' and 'functional' have stalked Huntingdon for most of its 80 years. It sits on the fringe of an unexceptional town that clings to the dubious distinction of having educated Oliver Cromwell, and exists precariously alongside the rushing

Huntingdon's course at Brampton.

A1, overflown by nerve-jangling jets from the nearby RAF stations. Pretty it is not.

Its proximity to London, 60 miles south, has always been an advantage and the A14 trunk road, which meets the A1 in sight of the stands, is another bonus. A dedicated access road to the track causes problems only after racing, when the decanting of a crowd on to a busy roundabout in rush hour causes inevitable delays. By then, though, the majority will at least feel calmed by an afternoon well spent.

One of the beauties of the place is that it is impossible to get lost. 'Compact' can be a damning word – in estate agent language it seeks to conceal the spaciousness of a broom cupboard – but for a country racetrack it may be a compliment. Huntingdon, reading from left to right from the stylish entry gate, has a parade ring, a betting block and a grandstand. No need for heavy walking shoes, then, or even a map in the **racecard**.

Plenty else to admire there, though, especially a handy device of numbering races on the edge of the pages for quick reference. Also, a decent guide to the catering outlets, which have made startling advances in recent years.

TRACK DETAILS

Right-handed flat track of 1 mile 4 furlongs with nine fences to a circuit and a 200-yard run-in.

CATERING

This is a noticeably classless course, where Essex Men meet the Gentlemen of Suffolk – and the ladies for that matter. Turn sharp left inside the main gate and enter a quaint brick structure grandly titled the Seafood and Champagne Bar. There is room for half a dozen tables occupied by men with military moustaches and spouses with formidable hats; the food is good – try the seafood chowder at £3.50 – and the cabaret beguiling.

For £39.95 a head, including admission, you can have a table for the day in the Peterborough Restaurant – ask for one by the window as the rest have no view.

Downmarket tastes are amply provided for, with a parade of hole-in-the-wall outlets selling pizza, baguettes, baked potatoes and a hog roast, while the canteenish Hurdles dispenses Newmarket sausage and mash to a devoted audience from the East End.

The bars were upgraded three years ago and are now outstanding, not least because care has been taken to create appropriate themes. Nobody rode this jumping course better than Steve Smith Eccles – I know this because he told me himself, frequently – and one bar is dedicated to him and his winners, though it was a bit short on whisky to be fully authentic.

The locally born Giffords, Josh and his late brother Macer, have a bar named after them, as does the urbane and recently retired Hugo Bevan, clerk of the

---

HOW TO GET THERE

By road: Just off A1, 21 miles north of Bedford, with excellent approach roads.
By rail: To Huntingdon station, then 2 miles by taxi.
Admission: Members £16, paddock £11, picnic car park £6.
Website: www.huntingdon-racecourse.com

---

course here for 26 years. Each occupies part of the first floor of the stand and has been cleverly designed with a tiered standing area by the window. It is a small thing but it shows someone is actually thinking of the spectator.

Not everything is so effective here – the parade ring is too narrow, the winner's enclosure absurdly small and the **car parks** can be a bog – but it is a friendly place with an active management and a proper jumping feel, exemplified by the spectacle of the open ditch directly in front of the stand.

HOTELS, PUBS AND RESTAURANTS

Mention of chain ownership is enough to have most genuine pub-lovers cringing but the Huntsbridge group of inns is significantly different – they may be run to a formula but only the quality is uniform. Three of the four hostelries are within easy striking distance of Huntingdon but the fourth, the flagship Old Bridge, is a famous landmark in the town itself. An 18th-century town house on the banks of the Ouse – the river that causes the racecourse such regular strife – the Old Bridge is a stylish place to stay and has a very good restaurant. My own favourite of the Huntsbridge pubs is the Three Horseshoes at Madingley, just outside Cambridge but easily accessed from the A14, while the Pheasant at Keyston, ten miles west on the A14, also serves high-quality food, this time in a charming thatched pub within an otherwise

unexceptional village. On the river at Holywell, a hamlet east of Huntingdon, the Old Ferry Boat is a decent pub with rooms, while Stukeleys Country Hotel near the course itself is a reliable alternative.

• **TOP TIP:** The Huntsbridge inns.

MARKS OUT OF TEN

Access	7
Car parking	6
Comfort and cleanliness	8
Scenery and surroundings	10
Staff attitude	8
Racecard and communication	8
Having a bet	7
Catering	8
Bars	9
Viewing and shelter	7

Total (out of 100) **70**
Ranked joint 29th out of 59

Hotels, pubs and restaurants
☆☆☆

KELSO

For most of us, racing in Scotland is like going on holiday and, with the possible exception of spring festival time at Perth, the sense of escapism is strongest at Kelso. This is such a remote place that its catchment population within a ten-mile radius is only half that of the next most isolated racecourse. Yet, in an engagingly homespun way, it thrives.

This is not a course for a whistle-stop dash, catching the first and beating the last. Kelso's lack of two-day meetings warrants urgent address but it is still worth finding the excuse to stay overnight. Relaxing rural hotels abound, and the morning brings a stroll on the time-warp cobbles of the market town and a patient drive across the River Tweed.

Golf and fishing bring the tourists here, yet many may only have heard of Kelso through the lilting tones of Bill McLaren, extolling the virtues of some hulking 18-stone prop from the Borders. Rugby is the next big thing to farming locally, but there is an evident passion for jump racing, too.

Kelso's crowds are consistently higher than a third of the nation's tracks. Moreover, this is a knowledgeable crowd, here for the horses more than the hooley. Hence the half-hourly throng around the pre-parade ring, shrewdly situated directly in front of the weighing-room.

Ostentation is outlawed. No point in coming here expecting tarmaced car parks or smartly uniformed staff or cutting-edge cuisine. This is country racing, thoughtfully refined. The **car park** can be a bog but has the attendance of smilingly helpful stewards; the **racecard** is only ordinary but has a two-colour design and a useful race-number guide.

Adverts around the paddock and conspicuously high prize money are further clues that this is a commercial venture, rightly unwilling to rest on its logistical laurels. Dress standards are relaxed and hip flasks passed around on the open roof of the 180-year-old stand which affords a clear view of the hillside monument to James Thomson, composer of 'Rule Britannia'.

A modern Thomson, course chairman David, is omnipresent, even taking the microphone for some chummy public address messages. It may not sound very professional but somehow it suits the environment. They brand themselves as 'Britain's friendliest course'; there is also a sign proclaiming it as a 'commended attraction' of the Scottish Tourist Board. Both are justifiable boasts.

Viewing is easy and unobstructed, which is just as well, for most of the 'stands' are low, shallow and reminiscent of non-league football grounds but for their tellingly elaborate pillars. Past the winning post, the steps of the corporate Younger Stand offer a spectacular head-on view.

CATERING

There is a lively market in the betting ring and a new Tote building oversees the paddock, as does the hidden delight of the course, a cosy cottage now doing business as Rosie's Bistro. There are racing murals on the walls, flowers on the tables and a three-course lunch that might typically be cock-a-leekie, followed by haggis, tatties and neeps, with ice cream for dessert, can be had for under £10.

Some of the facilities are primitive, none more so than a corrugated shed with a stone floor that serves as an alfresco bar. Even

The Berrymoss course at Kelso is the successor to those at Caverton Edge and Blakelaw.

HOW TO GET THERE

By road: The course is just outside of the town, reached via the A698.
By rail: Nearest station is Berwick-upon-Tweed, 23 miles north of Kelso.
Admission: Members £12 (weekdays), £15 (weekends), Tattersalls £7.

Website:
www.kelso-races.co.uk

this has been turned to advantage – they call it the Chicken Hutch and it is packed every meeting, notably with owners and trainers taking a rest from more pampered watering holes.

The Tattersalls Bar, where beer is only £2.10 a pint and whisky £1.45 a nip, has been recently repainted to stave off the worst of time's ravages but it is not a place to linger. Head instead for the steamy-windowed snuggery of the members' bar. Pasties and decent coffee are sold here but it is at its best in late afternoon, when the self-satisfied and the

TRACK DETAILS

Left-handed chase course of 1 mile 3 furlongs, with nine fences to a circuit and a testing 2 furlong run-in. Separate hurdles course.

sorrow-drowning come together with hot toddies in front of the open log fire. It is just like a lock-in at a privileged country house, and every bit as hard to get away.

HOTELS, PUBS AND RESTAURANTS

Racing features some way below golf and fishing as popular reasons for visiting Kelso but the varied attractions of this cobbled Borders town help ensure both quantity and quality of lodging. There are guest houses aplenty but some serious hotels, too. Ednam House, 100 yards from the town square on the banks of the Tweed, is a place you are most likely to encounter anglers but it has an attractively

MARKS OUT OF TEN

Access	7
Car parking	5
Comfort and cleanliness	7
Scenery and surroundings	9
Staff attitude	9
Racecard and communication	5
Having a bet	7
Catering	8
Bars	7
Viewing and shelter	8

Total (out of 100) 72
Ranked joint 17th out of 59

Hotels, pubs and restaurants
☆☆☆

homely atmosphere. Up a signifi-cant notch, the Roxburghe, three miles out of town, has everything for the country sportsman, a fine golf course included, but will cost considerably more. Scotland is only beginning to advance the theory of eating in pubs but the Queen's Head in Bridge Street is worth a try.

- **TOP TIP**: Roxburghe Hotel.

KEMPTON

Only a few years back, Kempton was a course of size, stature, history – and depressing decline. Its gritty suburban setting was matched by gloomy corridors, indifferent attitudes and a pervasive seediness that seemed to suit its small band of devotees but acted as an effective deterrent to everyone else. The transformation may be incomplete but it is already remarkable.

This is now a welcoming, well-appointed and conspicuously caring venue, where the management is not afraid to experiment in order to attract and retain customers – no easy business in cluttered southwest London.

A view of Kempton Park from the Weigh Inn.

Kempton has begun to market itself as 'the London racecourse', which may just be one of the few mistakes it has made in recent times. The benefit of London's vast audience potential is outweighed by both the amount of competition and the lack of neighbourhood identity on which most courses can depend.

It is not that Kempton stands in an especially undesirable area. An attractive stretch of the Thames runs behind the course

HOW TO GET THERE

By road: On A308 Kingston road, close to J1 of the M3.
By rail: Kempton Park, from London Waterloo.
Admission: Premier enclosure £15–£17, paddock £11–£13 (prices vary depending on meeting), Silver Ring £6.

Website: www.kempton.co.uk

and Hampton Court is nearby. Its more common approach, though, is off the M3, past factories and functional housing estates. Somehow it is more urban and artisan than its neighbour, Sandown Park, and therefore has to try twice as hard to please. The motorway, and its A316 extension towards Hammersmith, is, of course, an asset. Only the feeder roads into the car parks, inadequate on the biggest of days, make access anything but comfortable. Signposts are efficient and the **car parks**, mostly tarmaced and well organised, are a treat.

Staff are more polite and good-natured than of old, a remark that extends to an army of cleaners in 'Team Service' uniforms touring the stands during racing, dutifully picking up the plastic beer mugs, betting slips and sweet wrappers that are thrown away.

Only a fool would discard the Kempton **racecard**, not only because it costs £2 but because it is extremely good. The accompaniment is a pre-race tipping panel in the betting hall and a 'parade-ring host' presenting news and interviews through the afternoon. I know there are those who still regard ruminative silence as preferable between races but try selling that to the young generation.

CATERING

Punters, as opposed to horse-watchers, are pampered, the atmospheric betting ring complemented by a state-of-the-art Tote shop, a Coral big screen with seats and desks for studying 'away' races and even the novel Sporting Index Bar, with its bank of television screens, spread prices and, by way of relaxation, six decent wines by the glass.

In more than this one way, Kempton is a revelation in the neglected racecourse area of providing civilised drinks. It is well worth a wander to the Silver Ring, where the White Horse has an authentic pub feel and offers – this must be a racecourse record – three good beers on handpump, all at under £2 a pint.

What a shame, then, that the cheapest of the three – Greene King IPA at £1.70 – is not only restricted to the wholly inferior keg variety in the posher enclosures but is charged at £2.50, an inexcusable price, even for the pleasure of standing in the stylishly designed Premier enclosure.

It is here that Kempton have wrought the greatest changes, creating public areas so comfortable that many people do not move all afternoon. There is a bistro, offering two courses for £15, and a two-tier viewing restaurant that ranks among the finest in the land, even at £69 a head. What a change from the archaic lunch rooms that used to stand detached from the action, behind the stand.

Everything here is open-plan. Moving the parade ring and winner's enclosure behind the main stand created a central feature, enhanced by the creation of a weigh-in for the winning jockey, next to the

TRACK DETAILS

A right-handed track. There are ten fences to a circuit on the jumps course. A separate straight course cuts across the round track and is used for sprints.

113

paddock. It gives the first-time racegoer a sense of privileged involvement, and a desire to come again.

HOTELS, PUBS AND RESTAURANTS

It is a bold marketing ploy to call themselves 'the London racecourse' and it is justified by relativity. There is, though, a

---

MARKS OUT OF TEN

Access 7
Car parking 9
Comfort and cleanliness 8
Scenery and surroundings ... 4
Staff attitude 7
Racecard and
communication 9
Having a bet 9
Catering 8
Bars 8
Viewing and shelter 8

Total (out of 100) 77
Ranked joint 7th out of 59

Hotels, pubs and restaurants
☆

---

grim canyon between the buzz and bright lights of the West End and the industrial outskirts of Sunbury. This corridor of commuterland, where the M3 meets the A316 beneath the Heathrow flightpath, is one of those areas bereft of charm, so head left out of the racecourse gates instead. The Thames is Kempton's redemption – continue towards Hampton Court and the riverside is appealing, the pubs quite attractive. Hampton itself has the King's Arms; it also has the Carlton Mitre Hotel, a dauntingly expensive staging post with river frontage. Keeping south of the M3, Weybridge is an agreeable spot with a fine hotel (Oatlands Park) and a few reasonable pubs. There is, of course, always the alternative of overnighting in the West End, though the battle through the traffic will soon confirm this is not quite the kind of city racecourse Hong Kong provides with its spectacular Happy Valley track.

● **TOP TIP**: Hampton Court.

LEICESTER

At the rear of the Victorian timber grandstand at Leicester, a door carries a perplexing sign, announcing the room within as the 'Safety Control Office'. This is the kind of thing one expects at Wembley or Old Trafford, even at Cheltenham in the madness of March, but it is a fair while since this dowdy racecourse drew a number that could reasonably be called a crowd, let alone one that needed controlling.

Like the cricket ground near by, where Leicestershire played to acres of empty seats even when winning the county championship, the city's racing is appreciated by professionals far more than potential patrons.

Elaborate ironwork on Leicester's Victorian timber grandstand.

The old and the new can best be seen by the winners' enclosure.

The attendance figures for 2000 show Leicester 51st of the 59 courses, averaging a mere 1,748. Sometimes it seems there are as many owners and trainers here as paying customers, yet the course is central, accessible and far more welcoming than was once the case.

There is pastoral beauty nearby but Leicester is an unprepossessing place and its sporting venues suffer for it, sometimes wilfully. If, for instance, they demolished the ugly old number board and derelict centre-course buildings, even this course, hemmed in by busy roads and boxy houses, would not have such a depressing outlook.

The shame of it is that its discouraging image is now outdated. Significant advances have been made, some more obvious than others. They now stage decent racing in acceptable comfort and do it with a smile. The staff wear yellow bibs like motorway contractors but they are plentiful, friendly and helpful. Encounter them first in an efficient **car park**, with an area for disabled drivers next to the entrance. Collect a **racecard** on the way in – it is basic but, as an unusual example of value, free.

Bypass the primitive toilets by the gate, where there is barely room to squeeze in past stacked plastic chairs, and do not expect pizazz over the public address; it would be a fruitless wait.

CATERING

Instead, seek out the Quorn Room, up an unpromising flight of steps on the back of the old stand. This used to be a drab and desultory bar but has been transformed into a bright café with tasty savouries, good coffee and home-made flapjacks to die for.

A new stand, opened in 1997 by Frankie Dettori, is largely responsible for changing the feel of a day at Leicester. Lunch in the restaurant is £16.50 and they even serve a civilised afternoon tea.

Betting areas are a commendable feature. There were only 22 bookmakers present when I visited but the newly surfaced ring is deep and wide enough to accommodate three times as many. There are ample Tote outlets and so many television screens you need never wonder what is happening at the away meetings.

Unless, that is, you are adventurous enough to take in the best view on offer. To find it, walk past the stands and the children's play area on to a grass bank that provides a natural grandstand above the final fence. Go for the thrill, cure the prejudice.

HOTELS, PUBS AND RESTAURANTS

An award of a single star is not for anything in Leicester itself, for I have always found it the bleakest of towns to visit, even by East

TRACK DETAILS

Leicester is right-handed and rectangular in shape. The National Hunt course has ten fences per circuit.

117

HOW TO GET THERE

By road: The course is adjacent to the A6 (turn off at J21) at Oadby, 2 miles south of the city centre.
By rail: To Leicester; a bus services operates between the station and the course on race-days.
Admission: Club £13, Tattersalls £11, picnic car park £28 (four persons).

Website: www.leicester-racecourse.co.uk

MARKS OUT OF TEN

Access	8
Car parking	7
Comfort and cleanliness	6
Scenery and surroundings	4
Staff attitude	8
Racecard and communication	6
Having a bet	8
Catering	5
Bars	6
Viewing and shelter	8

Total (out of 100) **67**
Ranked joint 41st out of 59

Hotels, pubs and restaurants
☆

Midlands standards, unless you are in search of Indian food. It does have one charmer of a hotel, Belmont House in De Montfort Street, and I would heartily recommend this – and its bistro – ahead of the queue of usual suspects from the major chains. On the racecourse (south-east) side of town, though, the A6 soon takes you to some notably attractive villages (start in Great Glen) and thence to Market Harborough, where the Three Swans is a decent place to stay. The best spots in the vicinity involve a trek around the city ring road. The Quorn Country Hotel, close to Loughborough, maintains very high standards of food and accomodation in a rural setting, while the Crown at Old Dalby, a converted farmhouse with a lovely garden, tucked away just off the A6 ten miles out of town, is the best dining pub in the county.

- **TOP TIP**: The Crown at Old Dalby.

LINGFIELD

There are two views of the modern Lingfield, both of them extreme. Some use words such as enlightened, enterprising and enhanced to describe a facility predicated on the promise of year-round flat racing, no matter the quality. Others snort that it is a desecration of a charming, challenging National Hunt course.

The proponents of such dogma will never be reconciled but both sides, in a sense, are correct. Those who recall competitive jump racing in a green and pleasant land fully meriting the old label 'lovely Lingfield' are entitled to feel deprived. Equally, the punters who relish having a well-appointed, if less attractive, course racing twice a week all winter are justified in saying a requirement has been filled.

One thing is for sure – there is no turning back. Of its 58 meetings

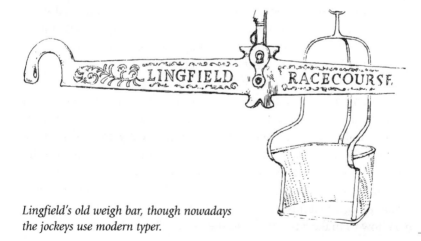

Lingfield's old weigh bar, though nowadays the jockeys use modern typer.

Lingfield: in the foreground is the Eclipse Suite.

in 2001 Lingfield offered only two days of jumping. There is flat racing on grass through the summer, some of it distinguished, but the core business of this track is now sand.

Through its owners, Arena Leisure, Lingfield has appointed itself the flagship of all-weather racing, and Arena shares have soared sufficiently on the potential for global Internet gambling to suggest it is on to a good thing. That does not guarantee customer satisfaction, but Lingfield has a loyal clientele and serves it well.

On winter Wednesdays there are unlikely to be more than 1,500 present and a course equipped for ten times that number can seem absurdly oversized. The advantage of this is the absence of queues and the ability to park where you like on the mostly gravel **car parks**.

Some days, staff almost outnumber spectators and along with the uniforms and the smiles they offer genuine service, from the muffled woman in the information kiosk to a sales and marketing office where a notice claims they will 'answer questions, and show beginners how to make a bet and read the racecard'.

In truth, the **racecard** does not need much reading. At £1.50, the racegoer is entitled to something more than a runners' guide with a few train times thrown in. Lingfield also skimps on razzmatazz around the winner's enclosure, but this is understandable when the winter racing is staged largely for betting shops.

Lingfield is a gambling course – why else would you watch moderate dirt-track racing? – and caters effectively, with a buzzy ring and an embarrassment of indoor betting facilities.

CATERING

Arena acknowledges the defects of winter flat racing (few want to come) and acts accordingly. Hence, affordable packages for hire of a private box and a £12 entrance charge that entitles you to roam anywhere. Many hardened campaigners start in the Derby Bar, where the stark, refectory feel is softened by a reliable all-day breakfast for £3.70.

There are two good alternatives in the brasserie, where both the hot pork baguettes and the patisserie are recommended, and the trackside carvery, serving lunch with a view of racing for £25 a head and full even on a chilly February day.

Racecourse bars rightly get a shocking name for complacency and incompetence but Lingfield scores highly with its half-bottles of champagne – for those narrowly deprived of a celebration – and quarter-bottles of drinkable French wine. The members' bar is decorated with

HOW TO GET THERE

By road: On the B2029, 21 miles from London. Accessible from the M25 (J6) and then the A22.
By rail: To Lingfield station, close to the racecourse.
Admission: Members £15, grandstand £12.

Website: www.lingfield-racecourse.co.uk

121

TRACK DETAILS

The round course is left-handed and nearly 1.5 miles long, with a climb to the start of the turn into the home straight.

caricatures, but a striking one of Henry Cecil is unlikely to be admired by the subject until the Derby trial meeting in May, when Lingfield changes character and becomes the place it used to be.

HOTELS, PUBS AND RESTAURANTS

This is a green and pleasant area of the Surrey-Sussex border country inhabited by city highfliers – and prices are correspondingly high. Much the nicest place to stay is the 16th-century Gravetye Manor, surrounded by 1,000 acres of woodland just outside East Grinstead; while it does not come cheap, it is also not beyond the pocket of many a regular racegoer. It also has a

MARKS OUT OF TEN

Access	6
Car parking	9
Comfort and cleanliness	6
Scenery and surroundings	8
Staff attitude	7
Racecard and communication	5
Having a bet	9
Catering	7
Bars	7
Viewing and shelter	7

Total (out of 100) 71
Ranked joint 23rd out of 59

Hotels, pubs and restaurants
☆☆

high-class restaurant. Pubs in the locality are plentiful, starting with the Hare and Hounds, handily placed in Lingfield itself, and the Blue Anchor in nearby Blindley Heath. Just off the A22, heading south from the M25, the Fox and Hounds at South Godstone serves Abbot ale, a good choice of wines and decent food in a lovely setting.

• **TOP TIP**: Gravetye Manor.

LUDLOW

The fertile imagination of P. G. Wodehouse positioned Blandings Castle and its delightfully dotty inhabitants in Shropshire and it often seems that they are all among the regulars at Ludlow. No racecourse more beguilingly combines flat-cap farmers and tweedy, cut-glass couples, while few, if any, exist in such a Wodehousian time warp.

This all helps to make Ludlow a singular venue. I know of many people who would number it among their favourite courses; I would

do so myself, for it is quaint, charming and quintessentially rural England. Looked at dispassionately, though, it is deficient in any number of fundamental areas that could be improved without risk of vandalising its character.

They have been racing here for almost 300 years and the place resounds with double-barrelled families whose ancestors doubt-

Looking out to Clee Hill from the elegance of Ludlow's grandstand.

123

Ludlow stands, looking northwards.

less attended the first meeting. The railway line that runs along the rear of the stand once transported the day's horses; now, it serves the less helpful purpose of preventing useful development, such as a proper access road and better **car park**.

This is a remote course, by racing standards, but only the most impatient will protest. The drive, from any direction, is enchanting and the local place names – Hayton's Bent, Hopton Cangeford – are a feature in themselves. Clee Hill looms over the course, contributing to one of the most picturesque backcloths.

The course sits alongside the A49, which avoids Ludlow itself, but make time for the detour if you have any feel for England's finest towns, or simply a yen for a good lunch. To the great good fortune of all residents and visitors, Ludlow has become a migrating ground for some of the country's best chefs and around their restaurants have grown characterful dining pubs of extraordinary quality.

Drag yourself away with time to spare before the first, because entrance roads have to cross the course and queues are routine. Staff are as rustic and timeless as the environment and the management, which has a sporting treasure on its hands here, could benefit from being more enterprising in such areas as the **racecard** – as basic as they come – and customer care. The public address resembles a list of parish notices and there is no course shop or information point.

The layout is, admittedly, a complication. The business area – paddock, winner's enclosure and weighing-room – is inside the track, which necessitates a half-hourly file of spectators back and forth on a well-laid crossing. As the average age of the regulars here is somewhat above that of, say, the Radio 1 audience, this is not an ideal idiosyncrasy.

Full credit, though, for installing a group of bookmakers between the paddock and the course crossing. Hitherto, it was a mighty dash to get a bet on after viewing the field, as I recall from the day I raced from the parade ring to hand over a good proportion of the week's wages

MARKS OUT OF TEN

Access 7
Car parking 7
Comfort and cleanliness 6
Scenery and surroundings .. 10
Staff attitude 5
Racecard and
communication 4
Having a bet 6
Catering 7
Bars 6
Viewing and shelter 6

Total (out of 100) **65**
Ranked joint 44th out of 59

Hotels, pubs and restaurants
☆☆☆☆☆

125

for the closest I shall ever come to a bank holiday coup. My unexposed hurdler, backed at 25-1, was beaten in a photo and I later sat in idyllic sunshine on Clee Hill and wept.

TRACK DETAILS

A sharp, right-handed, oval track. The chase course is 1.5 miles round, while the hurdles course runs round its outside.

CATERING

That was in the days before the Clive Pavilion, a spacious single-storey structure built in 1992 and now the focus of browsing and sluicing here. The bar is comfortable and well stocked but a touch expensive, with house champagne a prohibitive £27. The snack bar has well-filled rolls, soup from a tureen and home-made cakes.

The restaurant, where tables can be reserved for the day for £5 a head, is nice enough, with roast lunches at £10.95 and decent puddings, but there is no view, even of the paddock, and a disappointing lack of atmosphere. What a killing could be made here with a raised restaurant and the import of one of Ludlow's Michelin chefs on racedays.

In the meantime, we must be content with the Edwardian elegance of the antique grandstand – impractical and ill-equipped but impossible to dislike – and, best of all, the climb up wooden staircases to the wonderful Shropshire panorama offered from the open roof. Lord Emsworth would have heartily approved.

HOTELS, PUBS AND RESTAURANTS

The charm of the racecourse is its rusticity but there is nothing old-fashioned about the dining options in this remarkable little town. It is a strange truth that when one fashionable chef sets up in a place – even so out of the way a place as Shropshire –

HOW TO GET THERE

By road: The course is just off the A49, 2 miles north of the town.
By rail: To Ludlow.
Admission: Club £15, Tattersalls £10, course £5.

Website: www.ludlow-racecourse.co.uk

others will follow, and Ludlow now has the highest ratio of fine restaurants per inhabitant in Britain. As Ludlow, with its river and castle and general bonhomie, would be worth visiting if there was nothing more appetising than a few quaint antique shops and tearooms, this makes it a very special town indeed. Shaun Hill is the chef who sets the standards at the Merchant House Restaurant in Lower Corve Street, where those on a smaller budget can happily feast on top-notch pub food in the Unicorn next door. Picturesque Corve Street also houses Hibiscus, a newish, oak-panelled restaurant, while Mr Underhill's sits on the riverside at Dinham Weir. Overton Grange Hotel is a nice place to stay, as is Dinham Hall, opposite the castle, while two more outstanding pubs out of town are the Roebuck (top food and wines, decent rooms), just off the A49 at Brimfield, and the charming, creeper-covered Crown at Hopton Wafers on the Kidderminster road. Ludlow, sadly, has no two-day meetings but if you ever choose a racing town in which to spend a night or two of browsing and sluicing, this is it.

• **TOP TIP**: Stay the night.

MARKET RASEN

We are in that area of England where everything is flat except the place names, which are the most exotic and outlandish in the land. Go north from Holton cum Beckering, or east from Spital in the Street, to find the town of Market Rasen, famous for, well, for having a racecourse. And it is well worth the journey.

This has long been the only surviving track in Lincolnshire, a county – with apologies to supporters of Lincoln City, Grimsby Town and Scunthorpe United – that has no recognisable sporting identity. Market Rasen redeems the vacuum. It falls short of premiership standard because it seldom attracts the best horses, but everything else about it is progressive and impressive.

Although an exclusively National Hunt course, Market Rasen races through the year, the best of its fixtures falling over summer weekends. It led the objectors when Saturday evening racing was sacrificed to the Sunday crusade and managed to retain two meetings in May. Irish night and ladies' night will be justly popular.

The most striking thing here is that nobody haughtily assumes that humanity ends at the Silver Ring fence. The cheap enclosure staged a students' pink pig race at one meeting, along with more orthodox terrier racing and laser shooting. The area was crowded with folk of all ages and classes, here to be entertained and getting remarkable value for their £5 admission.

There is a picnic area, too, in the Silver Ring – one of the best around. **Cars park** with a fine view of the last fence and, unlike that other thriving country track, Uttoxeter, there is space to move. Space, indeed, is a feature of Market Rasen, even on busy Saturdays.

A corner at Market Rasen.

Nothing seems very busy on the roads in these parts, which is a bonus, and the course is signposted from miles distant. The fact that even the town signs bear a racehorse emblem is a hint about priorities, and once up the neatly hedged driveway there is an immediate sense of showtime.

The staff, many of them young, dress in green Market Rasen sweatshirts or fleeces. Smiles and courtesy from the gatemen are rare enough at British sporting venues to turn heads in surprise.

Racecards here used to be given away free; now they cost a reasonable £1 and are well designed, with editorial and good facility guides. As more courses sneak their prices up to £1.50 or even £2, those who hold at the £1 benchmark are to be applauded, especially when the product is attractive. Sadly, prices have now increased here too.

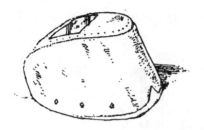

CATERING

The entry charge of £15 to members would be laughed at anywhere else in Europe, but otherwise this is a course that takes pity on the pocket. The food in the carpeted members' bar is fresh and cheap; coffee comes in civilised cafetieres. Upstairs, the Brocklesby Suite Restaurant disappoints in having no view of the racing.

The adjoining bar contained its quota of lads on a drinking

TRACK DETAILS

Sharp right-handed track of 1 mile 2 furlongs, with eight easy fences to a circuit and a 250-yard run-in.

The treasured hoof of 'Aly Sloper', winner of the Grand National at Aintree in 1915.

day out – hair cropped, shirts loose and voices raised. But with beer at £2.30 a pint and wine a reasonable £2 a glass, they were only enjoying themselves as much as everyone else. Soon enough, they descended on the lively and well-placed betting ring.

Some of the older buildings here still require attention but the management seems aware of this and is receptive to comments. Best of all its virtues

HOW TO GET THERE

By road: The course is 16 miles north-east of Lincoln on the A46.
By rail: King's Cross to Newark, then a taxi 1.5 miles to the course.
Admission: Members £15, Tattersalls £10, Silver Ring £5.

Website:
www.marketrasenraces.co.uk

is the bowl effect that means the horses, whether in the parade ring or on the course, are easily viewed from anywhere.

Pick a day, find a map and go – and if you come across Kirmond le Mire, you have missed it.

HOTELS, PUBS AND RESTAURANTS

Lincolnshire can seem featureless as well as just flat and the same might unkindly be said of its choice of pubs. The area is pleasant enough but there is not much worth getting here early for. Rasen itself is an uninspiring town for food and drink but six miles out, at Brandy Wharf – a place name of instant appeal to certain trainers and owners of repute – lies the Cider Centre, an idiosyncratic pub for scrumpy-lovers. For an overnight stay, the Limes Hotel in Market Rasen itself is a convenient option and you need to drive half an hour to find better.

MARKS OUT OF TEN	
Access	8
Car parking	7
Comfort and cleanliness	7
Scenery and surroundings	7
Staff attitude	9
Racecard and communication	9
Having a bet	8
Catering	7
Bars	6
Viewing and shelter	8
Total (out of 100)	**76**

Ranked joint 9th out of 59

Hotels, pubs and restaurants ☆

To the north, Winteringham Fields, near the Humber Bridge, is outstanding, while Washingborough Hall, east of Lincoln, belies its daunting name with friendly informality, spacious rooms and nice food, none of it overpriced.

• **TOP TIP**: Stay at Washingborough Hall.

MUSSELBURGH

It did not look promising. The angry clouds that had chased me round the Edinburgh ring road were now venting their wrath, turning the grass car park alongside the finishing straight into a quagmire. The distant Firth of Forth was obliterated by the downpour as the hardy, heroic and simply-have-tos picked their way through temporary entrances towards the dour and brooding stand. Perhaps I had chosen a bad day for Musselburgh; or a bad year.

Given a choice, the management of this compact, dual-purpose course in a civilised suburb six miles east of Edinburgh would doubtless have preferred me to come back next year. By then, they would have transformed both the facade and the facilities with a stylish new entrance building with bars, betting and weighing-room.

In the first week of the new century, they were making do – but not, I discovered, with the helpless sloth that retards many venues. There is a sense of energy and enterprise to this place, a clear desire to put on a show and make even the dank, discouraging days enjoyable.

Active since 1816, when beach racing at nearby Leith was abandoned, it is nowadays within minutes of the southbound A1 and the motorway network from Glasgow and the west.

Parking is convenient and free, albeit in a bog, and if the view through the rain looks mundane, there is actually a bird sanctuary on the reclaimed land dividing the course from the sea. Hemmed in to the left by grey stone houses, it is aesthetically agreeable and

Edinburgh's racecourse at Musselburgh looks across the Firth of Forth, beyond the stone houses, to the hills.

the track, tight and flat, is easily viewed from the single grandstand.

Facilities are limited by space, age and a history of disinterested management. This is a council course and it has not always been run as if racing matters to Edinburgh. The change is due to a positive committee, whose chairman, Pat O'Brien, might have been issuing a motto for the times when he said: 'Racing is all about people.' Bravo.

Musselburgh's crowds are up more than 500 a day in the past three years. Spectators are greeted by an attractive and informative **racecard** (£1) and a public address that boldly goes where many bigger courses are still slow to tread, interviewing jockeys and trainers between races. Entertainment, no less.

TRACK DETAILS

A right-handed oval of just over 1.25 miles, with eight fences (six hurdles) on a complete circuit.

CATERING

On a day damp enough to force most of the crowd indoors, comfort levels are stretched. Pinkies Bar, opened two years ago by Lester Piggott, is well decorated with racing memorabilia and has a line of television screens set into the wall above the bar. It is shoulder to shoulder in the queue for pints of McEwans (£1.90). Behind the stand, a brave effort to ease congestion with a 'Beer and Hot Toddy' marquee is ruined by a lack of mats between tarmac and tent.

Gourmets are thin on the ground at the eating end of Pinkies, judging by the number who ignore the fresh local haddock or excellent Scotch pies and opt for plates of chips. A small dining room with a handful of window tables serves a full lunch for £19.50 but the best tip for an afternoon snack is the Scottish shortbread.

The betting ring is crammed tight against the stand and, like most things here, would benefit from breathing space. The crowd was genial, though, the uniformed staff cordial and, as the sun emerged in late afternoon, I left in significantly better humour than I had arrived. This is a course with a heart.

HOW TO GET THERE

By road: Off the A1 to the east of Edinburgh.
By rail: To Waverly station (Edinburgh) or Musselburgh East. Bus service to the course.
Admission: Club stand £13; grandstand £7.

Website:
www.info@musselburgh-racecourse.co.uk

MARKS OUT OF TEN

Access 9
Car parking 6
Comfort and cleanliness 5
Scenery and surroundings ... 7
Staff attitude 8
Racecard and
communication 9
Having a bet 6
Catering 6
Bars 6
Viewing and shelter 7

Total (out of 100) **69**
Ranked joint 33rd out of 59

Hotels, pubs and restaurants
☆☆☆☆☆

HOTELS, PUBS AND RESTAURANTS

Perched on the very fringe of
Edinburgh, with a lovely stretch
of coastline to the east,
Musselburgh has an enviable
setting for those who want to
turn a raceday into a break. If
that sounds like a tourist
brochure, well, it's only what
the place deserves. Edinburgh's
dining-out spots are headed,
these days, by Restaurant Martin
Wishart on the Leith waterfront
but the choice is endless. So,
too, for hotels – Marriott,
Malmaison, Swallow, Sheraton
are all here but Holyrood
House, near the Royal Mile, is
the most stylish choice. Out of
the city, Houstoun House at
Upall is handy for the airport
and the M8 and has huge
rooms and a nice atmosphere,
while Roslin Glen, in a conser-
vation village south of the ring
road, is a relaxing spot. At
Gullane, a golfing village on the
coast, Greywalls (expensive)
and the Golf Inn (economy) are
recommended. Head east for
the best pubs, too, especially
the Tweeddale Arms at Gifford
and the Waterside at
Haddington.

• **TOP TIP**: Use the Houstoun
  House Hotel as a base.

NEWBURY

They have knocked down the Tattersalls stand at Newbury, probably just before it fell down of its own accord. It was never much of a draw, if you discounted the fish-and-chip bar at the rear. Keep a facility seedy and murky and you get the customers it deserves – and not many of them.

The point is, however, they have replaced this dispiriting relic with something modern and attractive. While they were doing it, a huge marquee was erected, equipped with carpets, patrolling litter-men and a bar with flowers and filter coffee on the counter. The cheaper end of the market is being served rather than shooed away. Newbury no longer has its nose in the air.

For all the natural eminence of a course that stages some of the year's principal races, both on the flat and over jumps, Newbury was not always an enjoyable place for the casual spectator. It was all too austere, too smug and self-important. The tweeds and old school ties were demonstrably in charge

The centrepiece of Newbury's older grandstand.

Newbury has some interesting betting stands.

and those of lesser influence or aspiration were made to feel like the great unwashed. The requirements were to park a distance away, tolerate haughtily unwelcoming staff and endure facilities decades out of date.

It took racing longer than it should to realise it had to compete for its crowds by giving them something other than a crumbling concrete step to stand on and a stale pork pie to eat, and, come the revolution, Newbury was not the quickest out of the starting gate. But the present management, led with genuine enthusiasm by Mark Kershaw, has not only absorbed the message but is advertising it well.

The attraction of Newbury for trainers is a track on which there are no devils and no excuses. For the spectator, the problems used to begin on exiting the M4 and joining a queue of shoppers and truckers that frequently tailed back two miles from the town, and end with having no proper view of the winner's enclosure – something else Kershaw is about to address. The seething at the wheel has been greatly reduced by the bypass, but Newbury is still a tough town to negotiate and its racecourse not the easiest to find.

Better signposts are needed, though this is the fault of the highways department rather than the racecourse. The easiest way in remains a cut through the labyrinthine back streets and over the old railway bridge. Easier still, if your starting point is London, catch the race train.

137

Factories and a gasometer dominate the rear view of the course and it still has some ugly, decayed buildings of its own. The main entrance is now imposing, though, and benches around a pond suggest care about appearance. More important, the stuffy officiousness has gone from the staff.

Newbury has a spacious, lively betting ring and plenty of other outlets that rise above the prohibitive seediness still prevalent in some betting areas.

CATERING

Bars are comfortable, even if the prices are steep, and the seven-year-old Berkshire Stand is the place to drink, eat and watch the racing. Built on five floors, with viewing decks and grandly railed staircases, it has both the look and the feel of an ocean liner.

In its short life it has undergone many changes and much criticism, not least about the lack of viewing seats, but Newbury now has two things right and those are the entrance

The spaciousness of Newbury's parade-ring area, and the attractive mix of old and new can be seen in this illustration.

hall, with its shops and information desk, and the first-floor engine room. Here, counters serve everything from a full breakfast to freshly made sandwiches and home-made cakes – a monument to modern racecourse catering.

TRACK DETAILS

Left-handed track nearly 2 miles round, with 11 fences to a circuit and a 255-yard run-in.

HOTELS, PUBS AND RESTAURANTS

There was a time, not so long ago, when you had to search long and hard to find agreeable pubs and hotels within striking distance of Newbury, and for an important course with a training centre so close, this was a considerable drawback. Happily, all is now transformed and the area is exceptionally well served, most

MARKS OUT OF TEN

Access 5
Car parking 7
Comfort and cleanliness 9
Scenery and surroundings ... 4
Staff attitude 8
Racecard and
communication 8
Having a bet 8
Catering 9
Bars 7
Viewing and shelter 7

Total (out of 100) 72
Ranked joint 17th out of 59

Hotels, pubs and restaurants
☆☆☆☆

HOW TO GET THERE

By road: From the west, leave M4 at J13 and take A34 into Newbury; from the east, leave M4 at J12 and take A4.
By rail: Paddington to Newbury Racecourse station.
Admission: Members £16–£30, grandstand £10–£15, picnic enclosure £4–£6 (prices vary depending on meeting).

Website: www.newbury-racecourse.co.uk

notably by the Vineyard Hotel and restaurant, very close to the course at Stockcross. Everyone agrees that the place is 'an experience', that the food is excellent and the rooms opulent. Naturally, it will also dent the wallet. Donnington Valley Hotel, just off the A34 heading south towards the town, is a handy alternative with the bonus of a golf course on site, but the best aspect of Newbury these days is the dining pubs close at hand. Charlie Brooks, formerly a trainer of this parish, now runs the Pheasant, just off the M4 at the Hungerford turn, but closer to the course are two outstanding eating inns – the Red House, just off the A4 at Marsh Benham, and the Royal Oak, hidden away to the north-east of Newbury in the village of Yattendon. With pubs like these, who needs restaurants?

• **TOP TIP**: Royal Oak, Yattendon.

NEWCASTLE

When Stan Clarke bought a controlling interest in Newcastle racecourse, his motives were not entirely sentimental. It was one thing to revive the grand old tradition of Blaydon Races and spruce up a place that had assumed the air of a neglected mausoleum, but the end game was to turn Gosforth Park into an all-purpose racing centre with the addition of a floodlit dirt track.

Clarke's ambition has been spiked by the curious reluctance of the British Horseracing Board fully to embrace the concept of night racing. And so, for the time being at least, he is left to make do with a busy programme on turf at a course that, despite its vast catchment area, had fallen into shameful disrepair.

Newcastle's weighing-room. Behind are stables with an 18th-centruy house at the end of the range.

141

The location of the old parade ring could make for some remoteness during actual racing.

Already, Newcastle has lifted its head from the depression. Close to the aptly named suburb of Wideopen, it is approached up a thickly hedged drive. There is the feel of a stately home but also the reek of decades of disregard. Suffragettes set fire to High Gosforth House in 1914 but racing survived; it almost met a much slower death at the hands of negligent management.

There are virtues to the setting, in a 1,000-acre park with its lake and woods, but Clarke has had to grapple with inherent problems too. The buildings were decaying, their grandeur long since surrendered, and the course does not offer natural theatre, owing to angle and distance from the stands and the trees that shield the runners in the back straight.

Those things that can be improved have received rapid attention. Clarke's beloved green paint and bold signs are evident everywhere but more profound renovations have so far cost £3 million. Whether this justifies charging £15 for a club badge on a mundane Monday is arguable. Crowds increased by an impressive 15 per cent in 1999 but dropped again in 2000.

Clarke demands high standards in two particular areas – staffing and toilets. The staff here are typically genial. I was ushered on to the grass **car parks** with such cheerful cries of 'champion' that I thought I had stumbled on to the set of a *Likely Lads* remake. As for the loos, investment is evident other than in the gents room in the original and elegant Brandling House, where the paint is chipped and the floors scarred.

Newcastle's **racecard** is excellent, albeit at the price of £1.50 that is now becoming a steep standard around the country, and the presentation here benefits from the decision to move the winner's enclosure to the front of the stands, where more people have easy access.

CATERING

The ground floor of the stand is a well-equipped betting area and foodhall. Typical of Clarke's courses it is branded throughout, so we have the Carvery (try the carved pork stotties – rolls to soft southerners – but not the execrable coffee), the Picnic Basket and the Nosebag.

The blackboard menu of the latter, and I kid you not, read as follows: pie and peas; pie and chips; pie, peas and chips. For something more adventurous, such as wild boar and pheasant pie at £9.50, walk down past the winning post to what looks like an old greenhouse. The Pavilion, open to all, is a brilliant conversion, offering decent food and drink plus proper coffee.

All the bars sell a choice of six wines in quarter-bottles at a reasonable £2.70 and the Brandling House Bar enterprisingly offers champagne by the glass at £4.50.

HOW TO GET THERE

By road: The track is 5 miles north of Newcastle on the A1.
By rail: To Newcastle Central, then metro and special bus or taxi (5 miles).
Admission: Club £15, Tattersalls £10, Silver Ring £5.
Website: www.newcastleracecourse.co.uk

143

TRACK DETAILS

Left-handed track of 1 mile 6 furlongs, with 11 fences to a circuit and a steady climb to the winning post.

The big disappointment, though, is that the beer on tap is a bitter from Yorkshire and a lager from Australia. Whatever would Bob and Terry make of that?

HOTELS, PUBS AND RESTAURANTS

Battle through the industrial outskirts into Newcastle itself and the city is evidently thriving, with a stack of trendy restaurants to be found around the renovated quayside. Hotels abound, too, with the Malmaison and the Copthorne offering reassuring facilities. Gosforth, site of the racecourse, is not so well served, even with the Swallow Hotel on the doorstep. Pubs worth visiting are in very short supply and it is worth detouring to the grandly

MARKS OUT OF TEN

Access 8
Car parking 6
Comfort and cleanliness 6
Scenery and surroundings ... 5
Staff attitude 7
Racecard and communication 6
Having a bet 7
Catering 8
Bars 8
Viewing and shelter 6

Total (out of 100) **67**
Ranked joint 41st out of 59

Hotels, pubs and restaurants
☆☆

named suburb of New York, just north of the Tyne tunnel, to drink Timothy Taylors and the locally brewed and evocatively labelled Mordue Workie Ticket ales at Shiremoor Farm. Just a mile north of the course, in Seaton Burn, lies the real find. Horton Grange Hotel is a country house with nine bedrooms and a fine conservatory restaurant.

• **TOP TIP**: Horton Grange Hotel.

NEWMARKET

No-one of sound mind, charged with creating a customer-friendly racecourse for the 21st century, would use Newmarket as an example – other than of what to avoid. It is not the structures or the standards that are out of step with modern requirements but the shape of the course itself, stretching away into infinity like a Roman road.

The charm of British racing is that each course bears its own viewing characteristics, but Newmarket's straight miles and dog-legs offer the very minimum of visible action. Dots on the horizon bob

The course may not be modern in design, but the new stands certainly are.

gradually closer and then flash past the stand. What on earth did we do before the big screens?

Trainers love it for its lack of guile and complexity, and I defer to any who maintain that it is still the purest test of a horse's ability to gallop. But we are talking consumer comforts and this is one defect that the most progressive of managements can do nothing about, except perhaps equip every spectator with a horse, so they can gallop alongside the races as happened in the earliest racing days here.

All that can be expected is that Newmarket glories in the tradition of its interminable Heath and creates a suitably impressive environment to support it. Well, two environments actually, for this is not so much one course in 59 as two in 60.

The Rowley Mile and July courses are neighbours and similarly conformed but their facilities have little in common, bar excellent access roads – better still for the July course which even avoids the fringes of town – and an army of well-trained staff, discouraging demeanour of old softened by blazers, badges and a willingness to help.

The July course is an elegant, evocative venue for summer racing, all thatch, timber, canvas and eccentricities like an ornamental fish

pond as the centrepiece of an otherwise downbeat bar. There is a pagoda near the paddock, for some reason, and the pre-parade ring, veiled by trees, retains the magic of a secret garden.

On the Rowley Mile, the spring and autumn course, words like stark and functional come closer to the descriptive mark but recent developments, culminating in the controversial Millennium grandstand, have updated if not uplifted.

From the outside, the new stand is showy but too small; there is an impression that the money ran out just before it could reach an adequate size. Inside, it offers the best Tattersalls facilities in the country, a fact shamefully lost in all the fuss about the higher levels, though the rebellious members do have a point about the shortage of quality space allocated to them. The success of the Champions' Gallery illustrates the market for top-range catering with a view.

Newmarket's **racecards** are commonly £2 but with their attractive covers, readable articles and colours for every race, this is a fair price. An informative PA system is occasionally augmented by jockeys' autograph sessions, and racing would benefit from more of these in creating the hero culture with the young that other sports tap into so much more.

Comfort levels inevitably suffer on the busiest of Saturdays and even the new stand could not prevent 2,000 Guineas day being something of a trial. The July course crowds, lazier and hazier than those next door, tend to filter into the ample marquees or the well-sited Pimm's and buck's fizz bars. Drink too much, though, and they have a problem – loos are in short supply.

Newmarket's July Course: on the left is the jockeys' ambulance, made by Cole & Sons in 1900.

Some come specifically for the popular 'Newmarket Nights', Friday evening meetings with live music, usually from a moderately recognisable act. The management, led by its energetic chairman, Peter Player, has broken free of conventional shackles and Player merits further credit for the Champions' meeting in October, an adornment for the dog-days of the flat season.

CATERING

Newmarket's catering is better than most without aspiring to great heights of originality – the sandwiches, for instance, make the heart sink. But I did like the conversion of a dowdy room in the July stand to a deli café with bright tablecloths and blackboard menus.

The bars can get rowdy – this is prime territory for London lads on a day out – so, on a midsummer day, retreat to the head-on stand, next to the stewards' box, for the most idiosyncratic view of a course that must forever live in the past.

HOTELS, PUBS AND RESTAURANTS

The town itself is a disappointment – the pubs are best avoided, the one high-street hotel seems in a permanently scaffolded state and the only restaurant worth knowing is the Caruso, a popular Italian near the

MARKS OUT OF TEN

Access	9
Car parking	8
Comfort and cleanliness	7
Scenery and surroundings	6
Staff attitude	8
Racecard and communication	8
Having a bet	7
Catering	7
Bars	8
Viewing and shelter	6

Total (out of 100) 74
Ranked joint 12th out of 59

Hotels, pubs and restaurants
☆☆☆☆

HOW TO GET THERE

By road: The courses are to the west of the town, off the A11 (J9 M11). The A14 and A45 also provide access.
By rail: To Newmarket or Cambridge.
Admission: Members £18–£30, grandstand and paddock £12–£15, family enclosure £4–£5 (prices vary depending on meeting).
Website: www.newmarketracecourses.co.uk

TRACK DETAILS

The Rowley Mile course is an exceptionally wide, galloping track. The July course is narrower, but also galloping in nature.

Bury Road roundabout. Many racing folk like to stay at Bedford Lodge, towards Stoute territory on the Bury Road, or at Swynford Paddocks, pleasantly set at Six Mile Bottom. My preference is to head along the Cambridge road to Stow Cum Quy, where the Quy Mill Hotel has some spacious rooms (also some very small ones), a pubby bar with real ales and a cosy bistro restaurant. This also leaves you well placed for an evening at the Three Horseshoes in Madingley, one of the country's best dining pubs. Heading east from Newmarket, the Angel at Bury St Edmunds and the Riverside at Mildenhall are good bases – also the idiosyncratic Worlington Hall just outside Mildenhall. At Fordham, the White Hart is a good dining pub in the same ownership as the Red Lion at Icklingham, where the food is good but the welcome a shade frosty if you mistake it for the pub it purports to be. After waiting for ten minutes at an unattended bar, and commenting on it, I was told: 'We're more a restaurant, really.' What pretensions.

- **TOP TIP:** Quy Mill Hotel and the Three Horseshoes, Madingley.

NEWTON ABBOT

Some courses make the best of their aesthetics, others make the best of their resources. And then there are those rare beings unblessed by such virtues who contrive to do pretty well in spite of everything.

Casual preconceptions of Newton Abbot would be misleading. Set as it is in the holiday land of south Devon, between the moors and the beaches, the mental picture is of a cosy, rural course with bucolic scenery. The reality, a mongrel of a venue, its access road snarled by do-it-yourself stores and supermarkets, comes as a disorientating shock.

Look left from the stand on to a scruffy greyhound track; look right on to a railway line. Straight ahead lies the dual carriageway to Torbay, escorted by pylons. It is not an outlook to inspire great thoughts, so it is just as well that the core product of the place lifts the spirits.

Every course must aspire to better racing and Newton Abbot has achieved a marked improvement in recent years. No track that started life as a sideshow to the local cheese-and-onion fair is likely to have ideas above its station but assertive management has enhanced sponsorship, and therefore prize money, by pursuing a dedicated policy of summer racing. This year, even the traditional Boxing Day meeting has been surrendered.

Of its 18 meetings in 2001, 13 will fall between the end of May and early September. If you've got it, flaunt it, and what Newton Abbot has is a captive audience of tourists looking for distraction. In years gone by, when the facilities were primitive, the discerning holidaymaker would have only come once but nowadays he may make it a diary date.

True, the descent to the course remains a retail and industrial maze, but the boundary walls and signs have been repainted and the entrance to the excellent **car parks** given a slick, businesslike air. Staff do not wear uniforms but are chummy and informed.

The **racecard** is poor, offering nothing above the essentials; as they set out to attract a passing market of the unconverted and uninitiated, this should be a priority. Paddock interviews are broadcast on the public address, however, and there is a quaint racecourse shop and information point.

Comfort levels have risen through small, thoughtful touches. There is a summer terrace with tables and chairs overlooking the paddock, lifts for the elderly and ramps and a raised viewing area for those in wheelchairs. The weighing-room remains a decrepit eyesore but is apparently next on the job list.

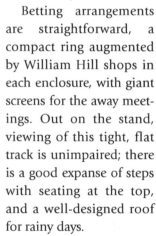

Betting arrangements are straightforward, a compact ring augmented by William Hill shops in each enclosure, with giant screens for the away meetings. Out on the stand, viewing of this tight, flat track is unimpaired; there is a good expanse of steps with seating at the top, and a well-designed roof for rainy days.

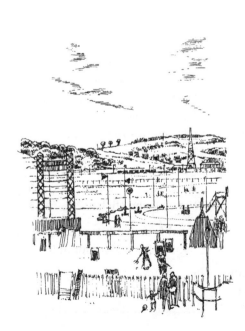

Newton Abbot racecourse has many other activities, which do not make for visual harmony.

151

TRACK DETAILS

A left-handed, flat, oval track of about 9 furlongs with a short run-in.

CATERING

Hedonism never sat easily with Newton Abbot. Years ago, it was here that I welcomed my first winner as an owner (I think there has been one since), and it was hard to know whether to begin the celebrations with a stale sausage roll in the grim snack bar beneath the stand or with a warm lager from the rudimentary bar.

Things are different now, and very much better. Most of the bars remain functional but the Red Rum, on the end of the stand, has been made into an atmospheric room, its walls covered in framed photos of bygone racedays. With beer at £2.20 per pint and Californian wine at £1.85 per glass, prices are realistic.

The catering is transformed. The stylish Terrace Room offers one, two or three courses with a view of the paddock. Set lunches in the Winning Post cost £29, with a decent wine list, but there will always be a scrap for the only two tables in the window with a proper view of racing.

Best of all is the large, democratic Manicou, a self-service eatery with ample tables, each

MARKS OUT OF TEN

Access	7
Car parking	8
Comfort and cleanliness	7
Scenery and surroundings	5
Staff attitude	7
Racecard and communication	5
Having a bet	8
Catering	8
Bars	6
Viewing and shelter	8

Total (out of 100) 69
Ranked joint 33rd out of 59

Hotels, pubs and restaurants
☆☆☆☆☆

By road: Off the A380, which runs south from the M5.
By rail: To Newton Abbot; a bus service runs to the racecourse.
Admission: Paddock £12, course £5.

Website:www.pmasterson @newtonabbotracing.com

of them bearing a flower decoration. If the little things matter, Newton Abbot knows how to win hearts.

HOTELS, PUBS AND RESTAURANTS

Proximity to Torbay ensures a holiday feel and the concentration on summer fixtures ensures that many of the crowd will be migrating from the hotels and guest houses of 'the English Riviera'. Whether

racegoers are wise to go in that direction for an overnighter is debatable, though the Osborne in Torquay (around the bay from the tackier parts of town) and the quaint Quayside at Brixham are both nice places to stay. For convenience and admirable leisure facilities, the Passage House Hotel, just off the road to the course in Kingsteignton, is difficult to beat. Also in Kingsteignton, tucked away in a residential street, is a very agreeable pub, the Old Rydon, where the lunches are good and the beer is London Pride. Other pubs worth knowing are the Church House at Stokeinteignhead and the Wild Goose at Combeteignhead, the latter especially good for real ales. Orestone Manor at Maidencombe, on the coast above Torquay, is another nice place to stay.

* **TOP TIP:** Old Rydon Inn, Kingsteignton.

153

NOTTINGHAM

After many years of mental torture, I have finally discovered the means of making a day at Nottingham races tolerably enjoyable. The early blindfold is the key. Apply it once over the River Trent (probably best if someone else is driving) and do not remove until inside the stands. The misery thus avoided is enough to make the remainder of the experience almost a treat.

There are certain handicaps that the most enlightened managements are powerless to overcome, and the most profound of them is setting. Nottingham is an enviable city, geographically and culturally, but this will be a mystery to those who know the place only by its racecourse.

It lurks in an industrial jungle of builders' merchants and car-repair units and, even when found, presents a grim face guaranteeing

instant lowering of spirits. Its entrance buildings are ancient and the rear of the main stand resembles a 1950s' public library. Viewed on a damp day – and it might be me, but it does always seem to rain at Nottingham – it is among the most uninviting sights in British racing.

Press on, though, for it really does get better. Nottingham is at the pinched end of the Racecourse Holdings Trust group but it is using available resources with enterprise. Its public areas, indeed, now compare favourably with far more illustrious settings for comfort and amenities.

CATERING

The old grandstand has been extended and redecorated and, crucially, a top-floor restaurant has recently been opened. It is limited in size but has half a dozen race-viewing tables and lunch at £35 a head.

Alongside, the eight-year-old Centenary Stand, royal blue with white railings, might almost be a jaunty ocean liner and is undeniably smart inside.

Food is decent – especially in the cosy seafood restaurant where the thick chowder at £2.95 hits the spot on colder days. Bar prices are generally reasonable, though keg bitter at £2.30 a pint is taking a liberty, and filter coffee is served at most of the catering outlets.

Some of the small things that mean so much – things that once seemed so depressingly neglected here – are also being addressed with interest. Signposts, both

Nottingham's course has the trees of Colwick Hill behind the stands.

across the city and through the tyre warehouses of Colwick, are admirably clear. The **car parks** are well surfaced and organised. Staff, smiling and polite, wear identifying jackets. An information point stands just inside the gates. Children have a safe play area.

Presentation has improved significantly. The **racecards**, quaintly sold by a man in a cloth cap and the woman supervising the cloakroom, cost £1.50 and include a track facts page and an editorial from the chairman. Between races, Graham Goode, the Channel 4 commentator and a director here, offers a chatty runners' guide on the public address.

With an average attendance of 1,630, this is not a course that is ever overcrowded but the loyal patrons respond to such services. They should also appreciate the improved appearance of the course.

Unless you stand beyond the winning post and gaze back at the trees on Colwick Hill, this is an irredeemably functional spot, but new flowerbeds and facility signs are among the features reflecting credit on the management team.

Most of the bars here are smart and Frankie's Bar even has a touch of style. In the Centenary Stand, the main social area has quarter-bottles of wine at £3.10 and leads out onto a covered balcony where the races can be watched in comfort. In truth, you

TRACK DETAILS

A left-handed oval track of 1.5 miles, largely flat, with a 4.5 furlong straight.

HOW TO GET THERE

By road: On the B686 at Colwick, east of the city. The course can be approached via the M1, A52 and A46.
By rail: To Nottingham, 2 miles from course.
Admission: Members £15, Tattersalls £10.

Website: www. nottinghamracecourse.co.uk

can watch in comfort from almost anywhere here, such is the flatness of the track and the sparseness of the crowds, but, once across that intimidating threshold, it is not quite the eyesore of old.

HOTELS, PUBS AND RESTAURANTS

You would not know it from the warehouses and car showrooms of Colwick, where the racecourse has the misfortune to be placed, but Nottingham is a city with plenty going for it. The aesthetic accoutrements of river and castle combine with a young feel to offer plenty of buzzy pubs and restaurants. Hotels let the town down – there are plenty of them but, almost without exception, the rooms are small and airless. Much the nicest spot is Des Clos Hotel, a farmhouse conversion on the riverside in Old Lenton Lane – the setting, under pylons and flyovers and accessed from a trading estate, is inauspicious, but inside all is tranquil and

MARKS OUT OF TEN	
Access	7
Car parking	7
Comfort and cleanliness	8
Scenery and surroundings	3
Staff attitude	8
Racecard and communication	7
Having a bet	7
Catering	7
Bars	7
Viewing and shelter	7
Total (out of 100)	69

Ranked joint 33rd out of 59

Hotels, pubs and restaurants
☆☆☆

spacious, with a fine restaurant as a bonus. Harts, a brasserie in the stylish Park Row quarter, is my favourite Nottingham eaterie and the best pub is the Lincolshire Poacher, a real ale-drinker's delight on the Mansfield Road. Out of town the Martins Arms, off the A46 at Colston Bassett, is one of the best dining pubs around.

● **TOP TIP**: Hotel Des Clos.

157

PERTH

John Francome remembers riding in an unusually delayed race at Perth. 'We were circling down at the start for ages, while the starter was up to his knees in the river, trying to catch a salmon', he relates. Now, Francome's stories can tend towards the tall but this one, illustrating the informality and natural assets of Perth, is recognisably authentic.

It is set in the grounds of Scone Palace, approached up a driveway fringed with ducks and pheasants. Its **car parks** must be among the most coveted picnic grounds in the land, its outlook is verdant and tranquil. And I discovered all this only at the third attempt.

Perth grandstand in the depths of winter.

The weather in Perth is always a consideration, but the jockeys are always willing to make the journey.

Having tried to attend the past two April festivals at the course, only to see all three days washed out on both occasions, I was relieved to be there when they could actually stage a race. For me, as for most of the population, Perth – 450 miles from London and the most northerly of our 59 varieties – requires forward planning.

Many pilgrims from the south, ranging from trainers through stable lads to besotted racegoers, become sworn converts to the charms of the place. The surrounding area is stunning, particularly for golfers and gourmets, and the racecourse has that priceless intangible, atmosphere. Like Cartmel, only different.

Fundamentally, this is a tiny, remote track and it could easily be an inconsequential one but for the passion of a small but energetic management team. The buildings are largely of low-rise timber, including a neat extension of the weighing-room block for offices and private boxes. The main exception, a nine-year-old function block beyond the winning post, was built in stone, but still in character.

CATERING

Unlike the majority of racecourses, Perth is free of aesthetic horrors. Even an unpromising stone shack, down the course, has been turned into a cheerful bar and named the Last Ditch. Parts of the old stand exist in a time warp but shabby decline is manfully resisted.

My few complaints are headed by poor signposting from the town and extend to two cases of overpricing. Whatever the many merits of Perth, it stages fundamentally moderate jump racing and £15 for a club badge is excessive. If the plea is economic justification, there can be none in the remarkable charge of £4.10 for a hot pork roll in the club bar.

Catering, to be frank, is not Perth's greatest selling point. The main restaurant is to the rear of the stand, a cosy room serving hearty carvery meals for around £10, but it has no racing feel. There is a well-staffed snack bar majoring on steak pies and fish and chips, but a viewing restaurant here would be a priceless enhancement.

For a course with a river running through it, space is a constant problem. The betting ring is cramped but an extra group of bookmakers has been placed by the paddock, which is the stage for Perth's admirable communication efforts.

They have only a modest **race-card** but this is compensated by a gossipy tipping session over the public address before racing and a diet of post-race interviews. Crowds linger round the paddock, a testimony to its success, and

---

HOW TO GET THERE

By road: Off A93, 3 miles north of Perth.
By rail: To Perth station, then taxi.
Admission: Club £15, paddock £8, course £4, picnic car park £10 (four persons).
Website: www.perth-races.co.uk

---

they even listen when the course manager, Sam Morshead, addresses them with the intimate loquaciousness of a country vicar giving the weekly sermon.

At Perth, you can drink a pint of beer or a glass of wine for only £2.10 and choose to sup it either in a padded armchair or while perusing the wonderful pictures of bygone racedays, kilts and sporrans aplenty. You can view every furlong of the course without obstruction, including the theatre of a water jump in front of the stand. The one warning is that it may suddenly seem a long way home, and you may not wish to leave.

HOTELS, PUBS AND RESTAURANTS

The loss to waterlogging of Perth's April festival for two successive years was a grievous blow to those familiar with the delights of this area, and although it did take place in 2001, inecessant rain made the racing hours, at least, a test of endurance. Perth stages plenty of summer racing, though, and there are few more congenial spots for a few nights away. Hotels range down in price and stature from the wonderful Gleneagles, which everyone should sample once, through a series of more modestly priced but comfortable bases both in Auchterarder and Perth itself, where the Murrayshall is a blissful spot with its own golf course. The

MARKS OUT OF TEN

Access 6
Car parking 8
Comfort and cleanliness 6
Scenery and surroundings ... 7
Staff attitude 8
Racecard and communication 7
Having a bet 6
Catering 6
Bars 7
Viewing and shelter 8

Total (out of 100) 71
Ranked joint 23rd out of 59

Hotels, pubs and restaurants
☆☆☆☆

concept of eating out, both in pubs and restaurants, is finding its feet in provincial Scotland and Perth has two related brasseries – Let's Eat and Let's Eat Again. For a pub with atmosphere, those staying over should head out to Glendevon and the Tormaukin Inn for good food and wine and Timothy Taylors beer.

• **TOP TIP**: Gleneagles (if the wallet allows).

161

PLUMPTON

There are courses for punters and courses for posers; Plumpton is a founder member of the former group. It is a place where the 'faces' of the ring descend on a winter Monday, spreading the word in muttered cockney rhyming slang. It is a place of informality, bordering on scruffiness, a place where Damon Runyon might have created a new character or two.

Just north of brassy Brighton, and a convenient station on the commuter train from Victoria, Plumpton attracts the accents and outlooks of the smoke. Its patrons, I suspect, used to revel in the seediness of it all. They once staged Bible weeks here, but these can surely only have been a vain attempt to convert the sinners.

A few years back, Plumpton was irredeemably crummy. Its facilities pandered to the lowest common denominator and Fred Winter thought the steeplechase track so treacherous that he refused to ride it. Only the feckless and reckless liked Plumpton.

A great deal has improved since those times. It will never be Ascot – gor blimey, the punters would rebel at such airs and graces – but it has become, through sensible investment and restructuring, a neat and purposeful racecourse.

It is owned these days by the chairman of the British Horseracing Board, Peter Savill, which may seem to some cynical souls akin to a master butcher promoting the cause of vegetarianism. Savill's well-chronicled distaste for certain racecourse administrators, though, does not preclude him from running a tight ship himself.

Enterprise fills the bracing East Sussex air, with bustling corporate boxes and advertising boards around the perimeter fence of the paddock. The Plumpton **racecard** is a fine example of a small course promoting itself – a bright, impressive production with excellent guides, and what is more comes free, included with the price of admission.

Runners leave the paddock here to a bugler's fanfare, a shameless steal from American racing and doubtless irritating to some. At least it is distinctive, though, something to identify Plumpton from the parade of similar, struggling low-grade tracks.

Some things still need urgent attention. Despite the valiant volume of yellow signs, it is hard enough to find Plumpton in the Bermuda triangle above Lewes, without then having to bump down a narrow, rutted track into the barely supervised bog of the main **car park**.

Staffing here can be unobtrusive almost to the point of invisible; there is a happy medium between officiousness and complacency and Plumpton falls just below it. Last of the gripes concerns shelter, which is pretty limited, with one Tattersalls stand completely uncovered. Roofs cost money that small courses cannot easily raise but this is a deterrent in midwinter.

Two beautiful oak trees grace the parade ring, and the course has the South Downs as a backcloth.

CATERING

Great strides have been made inside the stands, with new fixtures and fittings evident everywhere. All the bars are comfortable – none of the old hovels remains – though the charge of £2.50 for a standard-size glass of wine takes the edge off the impact.

The top-floor Paddock Restaurant is pleasant, airy and offers a view of the top part of the track from the dining tables. Earthier but atmospheric eating is done in the Southdown Fish Bar, where the splendid Barrie Cope presides over prawn curry, fish soup, fresh sandwiches and decent coffee.

Some of Plumpton's other catering claims are less convincing. The racecard describes the spacious Paddock Bar as a place for the 'not so hungry', which accurately indicated the spartan offerings, while the Lewes Bar is 'a wonderful, modern facility offering a range of light meals'. To my eyes, it was a counter in a low-ceilinged room boasting a single plate of plastic-wrapped sandwiches.

Most, though, come here to punt and they get their wish with an animated ring and state-of-the-art betting shops. Watch the helter-skelter descent of the back straight from the top of the main stand and, when racing is done,

TRACK DETAILS

Tight, undulating left-handed track of 1 mile 1 furlong, with seven fences to a circuit and a run-in of 200 yards.

HOW TO GET THERE

By road: Take A275 north of Lewes, then B2116; alternatively, use the M25, M23 and then A23.

By rail: From Victoria and London Bridge to Plumpton, then a short walk to the course.

Admission: Members £16, Tattersalls £12, Silver Ring £7.

Website: www.plumptonracecourse.co.uk

adjourn to one of many agreeable pubs in the picturesque villages nearby, all so hemmed in by the Downs that, blissfully, even mobile phones won't work.

HOTELS, PUBS AND RESTAURANTS

Sussex has always been among my favourite counties and this is a really fertile area for country pubs and hotel hideaways. Many of the surrounding villages have that cosy Englishness of tea-shops and vicarages that bring Miss Marple to mind, and it is worth ferretting out the jewels among the innumerable pubs. A few miles north at Fletching, the Griffin is a lovely place to stop for lunch, a pint or an overnighter. East of the course at Barcombe, the Anchor is a good riverside pub and, to the south, Juggs at Kingston near Lewes is a handy staging post from the Brighton direction. Closer still to the track, the Jolly Sportsman at East Chiltington is a food-

MARKS OUT OF TEN

Access	6
Car parking	3
Comfort and cleanliness	7
Scenery and surroundings	8
Staff attitude	5
Racecard and communication	8
Having a bet	9
Catering	7
Bars	7
Viewing and shelter	5

Total (out of 100) 65
Ranked joint 44th out of 59

Hotels, pubs and restaurants
☆☆☆☆

and-wine pub of distinction. Those wishing to stay down for a Plumpton fixture could choose Brighton but more convenient (though pricey) is Shelleys, a manor house in the middle of Lewes. Horsted Park at Uckfield and Newick Park Country Estate are still grander alternatives.

● **TOP TIP**: Jolly Sportsman, East Chiltington.

165

PONTEFRACT

Picture this scene and bottle it, for Pontefract is a structural and sociological marvel. Almost strangled by the blue collar of West Yorkshire industry and deafened by the hectic motorway that rushes above the back straight, a racecourse set on a prodigious hill contrives an improbable sanctuary, an urban idyll.

It is not, by any leap of imagination, the best of Britain's courses but in originality and atmosphere it is a match for all. There could hardly be a less propitious site – its landmarks are the M62, the belching chimneys of Ferrybridge power station, colliery gates and a churning roundabout. Turn sharp right into a park and enter a different world.

The ugliest racecourse approach in the country – also in need of more signs – is replaced by a council golf course and vast fields for **car parks**. It is raining as if the Ark will soon be required and it is a mundane Monday card, yet the place is buzzing.

This is a working man's track, so the day is imbued with escapism. It is as if Saturday has come early, though the evocative photographs in the members' stand tell of far greater crowds amid pre-war prosperity.

More recently, the course

The winning post is the best signpost at this course.

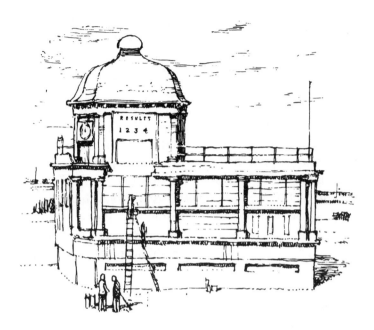

Pontefract's domed building opposite the stands.

could have perished like so much of the industry surrounding it. The spirit of such as Norman Gundill, its manager and general factotum, has ensured more than mere survival, for there is an air of ambition to the place that belies its physical handicaps.

Those who dabble in artistic imagery, exaggeratedly foreshortening a landscape, would find the job done for them here. Everything happens within a few yards of vertiginous slope. Jockeys climb up a path from the weighing-room to the paddock where horses plod, ready for the one-in-three incline on every circuit, while connections lean back to stop themselves toppling over.

If this is a study in miniature, the course itself is a startling contrast. Its two-mile circuit is among the biggest in Britain and hardly an

By road: North of the town, accessible from the M62 (J32) and then the A539.
By rail: To Pontefract Baghill, 1.5 miles from the course; or Tanshelf, which adjoins the park entrance.
Admission: Club £15, paddock £10, Second Ring £5.

Website: www.pontefract-races.co.uk

inch of it is on the level. It falls away from the stands, offering a vista best enjoyed in blinkers to block out the peripheral functionality, and the last three furlongs are relentlessly uphill.

CATERING

There is not enough shelter on the stands when the weather rebels, but try retreating beyond the winning post to the cover of a balcony outside the champagne bar. Here, heroic finishes are embellished by the muddied faces of jockeys and the heaving, squelching exhaustion of their mounts.

The club lounge has a fresh hot buffet, and coffee in cafetieres when the staff can find them. Upstairs, book lunch in a dining room that nourishes the racing atmosphere along with the appetite.

Past a shallow but active betting ring, the enclosure they term, with democratic delicacy, as 'Number Two' is actually the cheap ring but Pontefract has applied its standards throughout. The beer may be inexpensive, the clientele less affluent, but carpets and seating have been renewed and every room contains signs urging: 'Mind that cigarette – respect the furnishings.' Lest this sounds hostile, it is worth adding that the staff here appear to enjoy themselves as much as the punters.

Pontefract's **racecard** could do with a makeover, though at £1.50 it at least stretches to a glossy cover and map of facilities. Many tracks have demolished number boards and others, like Catterick, should

TRACK DETAILS

A stiff, undulating 2-mile course with a short uphill finishing straight.

follow suit, but here, in centre course, there is a domed masterpiece that must be preserved, along with the course it symbolically represents.

HOTELS, PUBS AND RESTAURANTS

To say the racecourse has more character than its surrounds would be a gross understatement. Historically, we are in pit country here and it is one of the most unprepossessing areas of Yorkshire, one that was never designed to attract those who wanted more than a pie and a pint. For respite from the traffic and industrial turmoil, head south on the A639 to Rogerthorpe Manor in Badsworth, or go three miles south on the A1 to Wentbridge

MARKS OUT OF TEN

Access	7
Car parking	7
Comfort and cleanliness	8
Scenery and surroundings	4
Staff attitude	8
Racecard and communication	7
Having a bet	7
Catering	8
Bars	7
Viewing and shelter	7

Total (out of 100) 70
Ranked joint 29th out of 59

Hotels, pubs and restaurants
☆

House. Both make good overnight bases, though many may prefer to go into Leeds for more choice in hotels and upmarket restaurants (Rascasse, Pool Court etc). As for pubs, cross the M62 from Pontefract and travel four miles north for the Chequers at Ledsham and its home-brewed Brown Cow bitter.

• **TOP TIP**: Stay overnight in Leeds.

169

REDCAR

Some racecourses are blessed by an approach road that quickens the pulse, lightening the dourest mood with a sense of anticipation. Breasting the summit of Cleeve Hill, for instance, with Cheltenham laid out below; winding through the Sussex Downs to Goodwood; or inching into the miniature market square at Cartmel.

And then there is Redcar, accessed from nondescript residential streets by a driveway with a graveyard to one side, allotments to the other and the chimneys of a chemical works belching noxious fumes straight ahead. Welcome to the Cleveland coast.

An exceptional racecourse would overcome such physical handicaps. But Redcar is exceptional only in its dinginess. There is a depressing air of waiting to be closed down, which would be the

kindest solution for all but those loyal patrons to whom it is the one source of local racing. Talk of uprooting the venue and creating a modern racecourse in the Cleveland Hills is welcome but, for now, Redcar must be judged by what it is.

First, the good news. It may seem a remote venue but there is good dual-carriageway access up to the final mile of 1960s' housing estates, which can be tortuous. The **car parks**, set on tarmac behind the entrance gate and in the popular centre course, are exemplary, as is the provision of disabled parking spaces against the rails and a children's play area in centre course. The signs are freshly painted in a hut by the Tattersalls bar that could almost be a museum piece. The staff are friendly with no false airs.

That is as far as I can go with the plaudits. True, I visited on a gloweringly grey afternoon with a thin crowd watching a thin card, but it was hard to find a scrap of evidence that things might look better if the sun shone, or that this is a suitable venue for Sunday racing.

Little things matter, a fact that has eluded the management here. An escalator ascends through the centre of the drab main stand and, at the top of it, the arresting images were of a rusting metal coat-stand, clearly a leftover from a 1960s' village hall, and an ancient, paint-spattered ladder leaning against the wall. What a way to capture the heart of the discerning sports-watcher.

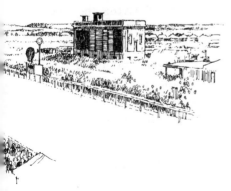

In the early days of the last century, Redcar's grandstand was a portable wooden structure, dismantled after each meeting. It could scarcely have looked worse than the eyesore built here in 1965, a monument to the crass architecture of its time. Charmlessness

Redcar has a magnificent straight mile which ends at the fine grandstand.

171

alone need not make it a bad facility but neglect most certainly does. My notes about the interior were succinct: 'Grubby. Rusting. Needs paint, or perhaps a bulldozer.'

CATERING

Comfort levels are consequently low and combine with the cheerless scenery in a distress signal that could be answered by welcoming bars and eating areas. Nice thought. The reality is rather different, though the Crows Nest Restaurant, with its two-tiered viewing tables, is an honourable exception. Here, at least, is the type of facility that every racecourse must now aspire to provide.

The remainder of the catering is uninspired, ranging from carvery baps at the members' bar to a self-service snack bar in the gloom under the Tattersalls stand, where hand-written menus extended admirably to a kids' range, even if it was chips with everything. Newer and brighter is a food and betting hall in Tattersalls with fast-food outlets for burgers, fried chicken and baked potatoes. There are bars at each end of

the hall where wine is a mere £1.40 a glass, though one sight of the huge, cheap bottles was enough to deter. A Pimm's bar by the paddock was boarded up, even on a July Sunday. It was not difficult to imagine the rest of the course following suit.

Paul Daniels is a native of these parts and visited the course last year. It will take rather more than his magic to transform it.

HOW TO GET THERE

By road: The track is 8 miles east of Middlesbrough; from the A1, take the A168, then the A19 and finally the A174 to Redcar.
By rail: To Redcar Central, close to the racecourse.
Admission: Club £14, Tattersalls £10, course £3.

Website:
www.redcarracing.co.uk

HOTELS, PUBS AND RESTAURANTS

Redcar itself is one of the more disagreeable seaside towns in the country and has virtually nothing to commend it in the dining and lodging departments. As most racegoers are arriving from the south, however, there are redeeming features near at hand. For a pub with atmosphere, not to mention a racing link, try the Ship at Saltburn, set among the fishing boats on the beach and a stone's throw from Mrs Reveley's mighty yet tiny yard. For a hotel with class and character, go 15 miles south on the A172 to Stokesley, where Chapters is very well run with an outstanding restaurant in-house. Alternatively, and for higher outlay, Crathorne Hall is close to Teeside airport. Chadwick's at Yarm is a nearby eating option and, some distance to the south-west of Redcar but on the homeward route for many, McCoy's Bistro at Staddlebridge has a terrific reputation and also offers rooms for the weary or emotional.

● **TOP TIP:** Chapters at Stokesley.

TRACK DETAILS

A narrow, left-handed oval track about 1.75 miles in extent, with a run-in of 5 furlongs.

MARKS OUT OF TEN

Access 6
Car parking 8
Comfort and cleanliness 3
Scenery and surroundings ... 2
Staff attitude 7
Racecard and
communication 5
Having a bet 6
Catering 5
Bars 5
Viewing and shelter 6

Total (out of 100) 54
Ranked 58th out of 59

Hotels, pubs and restaurants
☆☆

RIPON

We are in that prosperous, propertied part of Yorkshire where the vowels are not quite so thick and the peas not quite so mushy. North of genteel Harrogate but just a few miles from the A1, Ripon might be on a different planet, let alone in a different county, from some of its urban associates.

It calls itself the 'garden racecourse' and justifies the title with tidy lawns and a multitude of hanging baskets. It is also a course surrounded by, and even enclosing, water. A river lies to one side, a canal and marina to the other and a lake decorates centre course. It makes for such an agreeable setting that many will not trouble themselves over the dreariness of the buildings.

People identify Ripon with flowers and trees rather than dour, ageing red brick, which is a credit to the initiatives of a management doing its creative best against the ravages of time. This is a neat, compact course, fully deserving of an average attendance that puts it in the top quarter of British tracks.

The 5,200 median was comfortably exceeded on the Saturday

Ripon's parade ring is set among trees and flowers.

At Ripon the old Tote building is now the number board.

of my visit, which brought a measure of congestion to the approach road that winds from the A1, sadly without a single racecourse sign to reassure the uninitiated. Large, well-organised **car parks** and cheerful staff awaited.

It also brought, as summer Saturdays depressingly do, an excess of the crop-headed lager-swillers who practise their inane chants for the football season while forming a leering crush in racecourse bars. Not quite the Garden of Eden, then, though they considerately congregated in the Wakeman Bar, furthest from the track, watched over by good-natured security staff.

A few yards away lay a different world. Ripon has ingeniously recreated a Victorian bandstand and makes the best use of it. A Yorkshire brass band played through the afternoon and were giving such a haunting rendition of 'When the Stars Began to Fall' that a rapt audience on the encircling benches stirred only reluctantly for the first race.

They had missed the parade-ring pageant, another of Ripon's considerable charms. The paddock is a dominant feature, just inside the gates, and can be viewed from a variety of balconies. Tall trees rise in its centre as sentry and shelter, and there is a ramp for disabled racegoers direct from the paddock to a rostrum on the rails.

Nothing ambitious is ventured in a modest **racecard**, but Ripon sells its product well in other ways. Children are positively encouraged – this was the first track to have a playground and maintains an excellent kids' area in the Silver Ring.

175

CATERING

Everywhere, unpromising buildings have been turned to good advantage, so that one brick hut is brightly devoted to souvenirs and sweets and two shacks near the gates have become a cottagey champagne bar, complete with patio and parasols, and the Hornblower Bar, a more basic dispensary of beer, brightened by fresh paint and new seats.

A gloomy betting shop is out of character but compensated by plentiful televisions and Tote points around the course. The ring is deep and lively and the stands behind offer a compelling view of the business end of a race, as the track angles in towards the crowd, but barely adequate shelter if the weather turns bleak.

There is no viewing restaurant here, the main dining room looking back over the paddock instead, but the catering has ample variety. The Fountain Café has some imaginative chef's specials on its menu. The Paddock Café, with its cheerful apples-and-pears wallpaper, lost marks

HOW TO GET THERE

By road: The track is 2 miles from the town on the B6265.
By rail: To Harrogate or York, then bus to Ripon.
Admission: Club £15, Tattersalls £10, course £3.50.

Website: www.ripon-races.co.uk

by selling out of much of its hot food well before the first race.

Annual members have a bar with a view of racing but almost everyone can find a favourite drinking point here. For many, though, the pleasure of racing here will be enhanced by lunching first in one of England's most fertile areas for atmospheric dining pubs.

Personally, I can't wait to go back.

HOTELS, PUBS AND RESTAURANTS

Ripon is a pleasant town in its own right but the proximity of

MARKS OUT OF TEN

Access 6
Car parking 7
Comfort and cleanliness 8
Scenery and surroundings ... 9
Staff attitude 8
Racecard and
communication 6
Having a bet 7
Catering 7
Bars 7
Viewing and shelter 6

Total (out of 100) **71**
Ranked joint 23rd out of 59

Hotels, pubs and restaurants
☆☆☆☆☆

TRACK DETAILS

A right-handed oval of about
13 furlongs; there is a run-in
of 5 furlongs and a straight
6-furlong course.

Harrogate, which hovers not far behind Bath and Cheltenham for style and atmosphere, makes it a very good racing destination indeed. Not far to the west, the Dales offer quite different geography and a beguiling network of country pubs, of which the Red Lion at Burnsall is outstanding. You do not need to venture far from the racecourse, though, to find eating, drinking and lodging of very high quality. The Boar's Head, in the estate village of Ripley, has some lovely, spacious rooms and a pubby bar with a real ale – Crackshot – unique to the place. Harrogate has a bewildering choice of hotels but the Studley, in Swan Road, is reliably good. The drive north-west from Ripon up the A6108 is rewarding for both its scenery and the presence of the Blue Lion at East Witton. The brilliant Crab and Lobster at Asenby is only just across the A1 (though more in Thirsk territory), so the pub to aim for is the Malt Shovel in the village of Brearton, midway between Ripon and Harrogate – its food is so good you may struggle for a table.

• **TOP TIP**: Boar's Head, Ripley.

SALISBURY

Expect to encounter the impractical and the impoverished at Salisbury, for this is an ancient course in an inaccessible setting. It is not easy to find, can be maddeningly hard to get into and out of, and rewards those who arrive feeling irritable with cause for deepening hostility through some areas so tacky that it is wise to avert the eyes – even to the disagreeable caravan site behind.

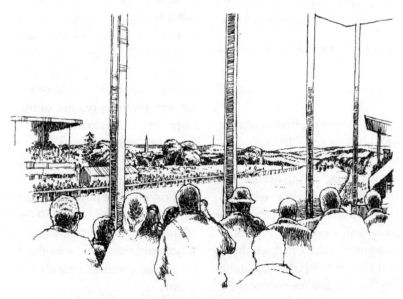

Stands border each side of the course at Salisbury, thought they do not prevent a distant glimpse of the cathedral.

Salisbury's old Rubbing House.

Do not despair, though, for Salisbury is redeemed by the unexpected – the clubby alcoves and patios, the freshness of the food, the novelty of decent beer on draught and, best of all, the long but fulfilling climb to the top terrace of the old Tattersalls stand that affords an inspiring vista not just of the racing, but the city and cathedral spire beyond.

This is a place that reeks of history and breeding, a place where Queen Elizabeth I is said to have visited as far back as the year of the Spanish Armada. That it has also developed a whiff of underfunding is evidenced by a decrepit and unusable Silver Ring stand and a pervasive shabbiness down the course, where even a modest injection of paint and polish would help.

A shame, this, because in other ways Salisbury is beguiling, a provincial track in enviable setting that could – and doubtless does – very easily become a favourite haunt. It is the Wincanton of the flat, with a similar feel and a similar clientele, at its best on a golden summer's evening. Its racing is invariably informative but the course is idiosyncratic, featuring a loop at its farthest extremity and – like the similarly shaped Hamilton – starting its long-distance races the wrong way down the finishing straight.

Strangers should leave ample time to negotiate the city, where signposts for the course are conspicuously few, and then the winding, narrow hill (a prolonged penance after racing) to the **car parks**. These are well ordered, supervised by watchful staff and feature some lovely picnic spots among the trees on the inside of the course.

The business area is intimate and informal, a parade ring shoehorned atmospherically between the main entrance gates, the rail and finishing post, the pubby patio of the Wessex Bar and an attractive weighing-room. The scene is completed by an effective if unattractive structure that serves seafood and doubles as a covered viewing terrace for the paddock.

Salisbury has belatedly begun to improve its **racecards** but it has not done much to enliven the old-fashioned décor and layout of the Bibury Room, the main social area within a stand with a graceful staircase and a sense of dated charm.

CATERING

The rare discovery on a racecourse of Ringwood handpumped bitter is made in the Bibury Room, while downstairs in the cosier Wessex Bar there is a decent choice of wines. Salisbury scores on enterprise here, rising above the laziness of so many other courses who provide bog-standard keg beers and predictably poor wine.

Catering is also a virtue. The Wessex Bar sells generous baps, home-made cakes and proper coffee and the Tattersalls bar – primitive but stopping short of shabby – is a pleasant surprise, with its home-made steak-and-

kidney pie and fresh vegetables. The main restaurant faces backwards, its view the caravan site, but credit to Salisbury for

HOW TO GET THERE

By road: The course is situated 3 miles west of Salisbury, between the A354 and the A3094.
By rail: To Salisbury, then bus or taxi to course.
Admission: Members £15, Tattersalls £10, course £5.

Website:
www.salisburyracecourse.co.uk

adding a clever conservatory extension, where a set meal at a table overlooking the parade ring is worth its price of £35.

HOTELS, PUBS AND RESTAURANTS

This cathedral city falls short on style in the hotel department, most of the centrally situated places being disappointingly corporate in feel. The Rose and Crown has a nice riverside setting reflected by its high prices, so it is better by far to head nine miles west of town to the picture-postcard village of Teffont Evias and its small but memorable country hotel, Howard's House. This may also be the best place to eat in the vicinity, though on the southern side of Salisbury the Three Lions

at Stuckton, near Fordingbridge, is a dining pub that runs it close. There are some characterful old pubs in the city, notably the Haunch of Venison and the unusually no-smoking New Inn, while the Queen's Arms at Broad Chalke and the thatched Victoria and Albert at Netherhampton are very convenient for the course.

* **TOP TIP**: Howard's House Hotel.

MARKS OUT OF TEN

Access	4
Car parking	7
Comfort and cleanliness	6
Scenery and surroundings	8
Staff attitude	8
Racecard and communication	5
Having a bet	6
Catering	8
Bars	9
Viewing and shelter	7
Total (out of 100)	**68**

Ranked joint 38th out of 59

Hotels, pubs and restaurants
☆☆☆

TRACK DETAILS

Right-handed track with a run-in of 7 furlongs. The last 5 furlongs are uphill.

SANDOWN

Sandown Park can be compared to Lord's or Highbury; it is a premiership course, moneyed and influential, so there should be few excuses for getting things wrong. Such élite tracks, operating chiefly on weekends and evenings to maximise crowds, are the shop window of British racing and must be judged accordingly strictly.

Despite a few wrinkles that need attention, Sandown stands the test well. This is a turbulent time for the headquarters of the United

The back of Sandown Park's grandstand has a viewing terrace for the parade ring.

The entrance to Sandown features gates that once stood outside the house of the riotous Baron Grant.

Racecourses group, awaiting the completion of significant redevelopment, but it remains one of the most enjoyable places in Britain to watch racing. I say watch, rather than go, because the downside of Sandown can lie in the frustrations of travel.

Sited so close to London and the M25, Sandown's apparent accessibility is a fraud. On Whitbread day last year, the final mile through Esher took me more than an hour, which can cloud the sunniest pre-race disposition. Even on lesser mid-week days, the evening traffic is so chaotic that many skip the last race. It is a shame, but I offer no magic cure, for this is cluttered suburbia.

Sandown, which started life as a medieval priory, offers a racecourse station adjacent to the back straight but those who conquer Esher in the car can **park** on good, well-organised surfaces. The entrances are slickly run by staff in blazers and badges, whose demeanour is notably friendlier than of old, and a jazz band inside the gates provides the first of several musical sideshows.

Racecards vary in quality, though not in price. For £2, the spectator is entitled to a production that entertains as well as informs – Sandown on Tolworth Hurdle day scored highly only for the latter, 183

Outside the weighing-room at Sandown a standard is preserved. In the background the spire of Esher church can be seen.

with its maps, guides and form. The Whitbread card, by comparison, was superb, intermingled with articles bringing the racing to life in a way that should not be beyond any leading course.

Communication is a strength. Sandown's public address is excellent and frequently broadcasts a panel discussion of the day's card before racing. A few more interviews with jockeys would not go amiss if they wish to build upon the noticeably young element attracted on Saturdays.

Esher Hall is where everything happens. Taking up the ground floor of the massive grandstand, built in 1973 and overdue for modernisation, it contains two spacious, indoor betting areas to complement the deep bookmakers' ring outside, so even when the crowds are at their biggest it does not strain time or temper to get a bet on.

HOW TO GET THERE

By road: The course is at Esher, off the A3 London-Portsmouth road.
By rail: To Esher, then short walk to the course.
Admission: Club £17–£30, grandstand £11–£20 (prices vary depending on meeting), Park enclosure £5.

Website: www.sandown.co.uk

CATERING

Sustenance is varied and plentiful, ranging from the mobile fast-food units by the parade ring to the Claremont Restaurant on the second floor, where lunch costs about £30. There are two seafood outlets run by the excellent Barrie Cope, and Mahony's Bar serves Irish stew and soda bread at £4 a plate, to soak up the Guinness. The Tack and Saddle area resembles a mini-motorway services, and the full breakfasts at £5.25 are a

TRACK DETAILS

A right-handed oval course of 13 furlongs, with 11 fences and a run-in of 1 furlong.

godsend before a winter midday start.

There are plenty of places to have a drink but, sadly, the members' viewing bar on the first floor is the most unpleasant and needs a revamp. Adequate house wine is generally served in quarter-bottles at £3.40 but the Café Normandie takes a liberty by charging £2.85 for a glass of the most basic plonk out of a machine.

Cleaners work to keep the place tidy but the toilets could do with more permanent care on busy days – nobody wants to wade across a floor of floods and paper towels.

The thing about Sandown, however, is its racing theatre. Follow the horses along the walkway under the trees on to the course, then take a spot on the stand for the finest view in

185

British racing. Forget the panorama of outer London and enjoy the best spectacle jumping has to offer.

HOTELS, PUBS AND RESTAURANTS

Esher may be a pig of a place to negotiate when you are late for the first race on a Saturday afternoon or struggling away from the last on a Friday evening, but its upmarket feel sets Sandown apart from its sister track at Kempton. There are some decent pubs in the town, especially the Wheatsheaf, up a side street on the picturesque village green, while the Bear, alongside the teeming traffic lights junction in the centre, is a popular pre-race venue for its cavernous bars and Young's ale. Back towards the A3/M25 junction, the Cricketers at Cobham is another decent pub and Cobham also has the functional Hilton Hotel for

MARKS OUT OF TEN	
Access	6
Car parking	8
Comfort and cleanliness	7
Scenery and surroundings	6
Staff attitude	8
Racecard and communication	8
Having a bet	9
Catering	8
Bars	8
Viewing and shelter	10
Total (out of 100)	**78**

Ranked 6th out of 59

Hotels, pubs and restaurants
☆☆☆

overnight stays. Swanky villages like Claygate are always likely to have some fashionable eateries and Le Petit Pierrot fits the bill, though Esher itself has a good range of cafés and restaurants.

● **TOP TIP:** Wheatsheaf pub on the green.

SEDGEFIELD

The unwitting visitor to Sedgefield racecourse may consider it a prize unlikely to provoke a lengthy court battle, yet the second incursion of Sir Stanley Clarke's empire into the north-east encountered stout legal resistance from one traditional shareholder, presumably set against the green paint, band music and general popularising of the Clarke regime.

Sir Stan has evidently won the day and his past form, invigorating such dowdy venues as Uttoxeter and Brighton, warns against scepticism. Sedgefield, though, will present a stern and singular challenge.

Sedgefield's looks have improved considerably; the following pages show how it once was.

It is not in decline – indeed, the management of recent years has been notably enterprising – and nor, despite first appearances, is it begging for change.

The branding here is 'the friendly racecourse'. It draws a hearty jumping crowd, not of the monied, tweedy variety but earthy and working class. Close to Tyneside, it is nevertheless farming country. Sheep gaze balefully from centre course, and the sense of rural remoteness contrives to survive being within sight of the A1.

This, of course, guarantees easy access, further expedited by admirable brown signs both from the main road and around the quiet village. The **car parks**, one properly surfaced and two in fields, decant everyone on to a single narrow road, which can make departure rather more chaotic.

The locals may be friendly but there is no great sense of welcome at the gates. On a cold winter day, indeed, the staff appeared indifferent almost to the point of invisibility. The public address was no help, giving only the basic essentials, a comment equally applicable to the **racecard**.

Some would say that is the point and the appeal of places like Sedgefield, that the companionship of such country courses has no need of artificial aids. Here, I am with Clarke. Every course needs to show it cares, from the instant

The first corner at Sedgefield used to be narrow enough to cause collisions.

impression at the entrances and the words in the racecard through to the more lasting memories of eating, drinking and betting.

CATERING

Thankfully, Sedgefield is worth perseverance. It has its primitive relics, none more evocative than the Durham Edition Bar, where the ceiling is low, the windows misted and old men sit around bar fires peering at the *Daily Mirror*. The Pavilion, a building opened ten years ago by a local MP named Blair, is a different world.

Recent efforts to improve the catering outlets have produced an unexpected treat in a galleried viewing restaurant. It is small, nicely furnished and has a fine view across the course. Lunch is £18.50 and the restaurant is full, which should be a lesson to other racecourses

TRACK DETAILS

Sharp, undulating left-handed track, 1 mile 2 furlongs long, with eight fences to a circuit and a run-in of 220 yards.

MARKS OUT OF TEN

Access 9
Car parking 6
Comfort and cleanliness 6
Scenery and surroundings ... 7
Staff attitude 5
Racecard and
communication 3
Having a bet 8
Catering 7
Bars 5
Viewing and shelter 6

Total (out of 100) 62
Ranked joint 50th out of 59

Hotels, pubs and restaurants
☆

reluctant to invest in this most sought-after of race-watching commodities.

Elsewhere, the bar at the top of the Paddock Stand is worth seeking out, not only for a decent snack menu and pots of proper coffee but also because it is easily the most hospitable of a pretty uninspiring bunch. At the other end of the scale, in the bland Theakston Suite, stands a public bar so functional and devoid of racing feel that it could be a village hall. The bitter is keg, the lager Australian and the wine revolting.

A smart weighing-room block is among the recent additions but the previous inadequate structure near the main gate is now redundant, when it could be converted providentially into, say, a fish bar.

Sedgefield is neither pretentious nor élitist. There is only one entrance price and nowhere is off limits. Regulars will know to avoid the Dickensian toilet block but, on the whole, the comforts of the place are far greater than seemed possible ten or 20 years ago.

At its heart is a betting ring cleverly raised and separated from the paddock concourse by steps that, in turn, give an unusual and compelling head-on view of the home straight, which runs steadily downhill until the imposition of a sharp climb through the final 100 yards.

Watching weary but willing chasers ascend that last hill is the key to enjoying Sedgefield, even when the wind makes it feel one of the bleakest corners of racingdom.

HOTELS, PUBS AND RESTAURANTS

I could begin to feel bad about awarding only one star, because Sedgefield is neither an unattractive nor an unfriendly place. It cannot be argued, though, that its options for eating and lodging are anything but very confined. One might say, in fact, that they begin and end with the Dun Cow pub, which is within walking

---

HOW TO GET THERE

By road: Just off the A1(M) via the A689.
By rail: To Darlington, then taxi 8 miles to course.
Admission: Paddock £10, course £3.

Website:
www.sedgefield-racecourse.com

---

distance of the course gates and serves Theakston and Castle Eden ale and fresh fish lunches – a very decent local. That apart, the Seven Stars at Shincliffe is ten miles north and worth investigating, while those wishing to stay overnight might try the parkland setting of Hardwick Hall, close to the course, or head west a few miles for the Eden Arms at Rushyford or Redworth Hall, near Newton Aycliffe.

• **TOP TIP**: Dun Cow pub.

191

SOUTHWELL

Southwell is a diverting spot for historians, a decent base for forest ramblers and the ideal self-indulgence for inveterate gamblers. The course has 63 meetings scheduled in 2001, sometimes in binges of three per week, and it serves a kindly purpose for those who cannot get by without a bet.

The rest of us may loftily ignore the place, and most do. Southwell's crowds are the worst in Britain and, while this casts improper aspersions on an unexceptionable minster town, it says

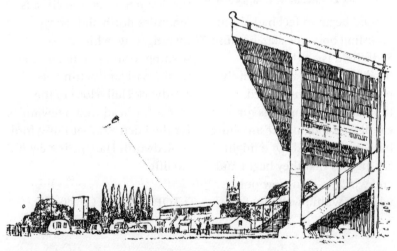

The view looking towards the finish and parade ring, with the tower of Rolleston's church beyond the old club.

everything necessary about the product. The finances of racing dictate a need for staging dirt-track racing of inevitably dire quality, especially amid fickle winter weather, but when combined with a sterile, soulless atmosphere, it is best left to the addicts.

If it sometimes seems that most of the spectators here know each other personally, it is hardly surprising. These are the diehards, their easily counted numbers (average 869) swelled only by trainers and owners, often arriving late and some looking faintly furtive, as if ashamed that the dreams of Ascot, Goodwood, even Dubai, have come to this.

Of all the 59 racing venues, a day at Southwell generates the least cause for anticipation. Elsewhere, even the crummiest of courses offer consolations – Worcester has its cathedral and river, even Redcar has the sea. Southwell has a rumbling railway line and a hazy vista of pylons.

Further afield, the banks of the Trent provide some cheering hostelries and the sprightly city of Nottingham is nearby. All is not quite lost. Southwell, though, is flat and featureless and functional; I even preferred it when it was a low-grade jumps course with facilities so barren that the Saracen's Head in the town took all the lunch business.

These days, appropriately, it is approached up a two-mile drive that seems sure to end in an industrial estate. In a sense, so it does.

Credit is due for the clear and frequent signposts guiding motorists through winding approach roads and for the optimistic scope of the **car park**. Members get to park on tarmac, right by the main gate.

There is no need to leave extra time for reading the **racecard** here, because it is nothing more than a glorified numbers sheet. There is also no effort to inform with news or interviews over the public address. You can see why, of course, but maybe the stands would not be quite so yawningly empty if the entertainment – for that is what it must purport to be – was enlivened just a shade.

193

HOW TO GET THERE

By road: Five miles west of Newark via A617.
By rail: To Newark North Gate, then connecting train to Rolleston Junction (adjoining course) or 4 miles by taxi.
Admission: Members £14, Tattersalls £8.

Website: www.southwellracecourse.co.uk

CATERING

At first sight, £14 seems a lot to pay for a member's badge here, but it is worth the supplement for the bar and restaurant on the first floor of the stand. Ron Muddle knew what he was doing when he bought this course and created its central facility, and it remains a civilised haven.

Lunch is £19.95 from a regularly changing and agreeable menu, with a good wine list, and several window tables look directly down on the finish. The smart bar is well staffed and stocked, there are ample tables and, crucially, windows and balconies on both sides to view the paddock and track respectively.

Those who pay only £8 have the run of the ground floor, which is well designed but on a more frugal level. There are circular bars at each end, one combining a carvery stall and the other a hearty if greasy breakfast bar. In between stands a spacious betting hall, where the regular faces convene to exchange good things for the six-furlong seller.

This is not a complacent place. Cleaners patrol the stand during racing, smart signposts direct the uninitiated and the lawns around the paddock are well

TRACK DETAILS

Left-handed turf course, 1 mile 1 furlong, with seven easy jumps per circuit. A round, left-handed all-weather fibresand track runs outside the turf course.

kept. A log fire burns in the owners' and trainers' bar and, in an adjoining timber shack of no obvious appeal, the Pantry is a welcoming retreat, with snack lunches and decent coffee and cakes.

The abiding impression, though, is of an undistinguished course, meeting a need rather than attracting an audience. Near the entrance stands the racecourse motel. It has only 12 rooms but that is probably plenty.

HOTELS, PUBS AND RESTAURANTS

There is an anonymous feel to the countryside in this area where Nottinghamshire meets Lincolnshire in a convergence of trunk roads, and the best that can be said of the social opportunities is that the nearby Trent affords some attractively isolated riverside pubs in villages such as Gunthorpe and Bleasby. Much the best option in the locality lies closer to the racecourse at Upton, on the A612, where the

MARKS OUT OF TEN	
Access	7
Car parking	7
Comfort and cleanliness	7
Scenery and surroundings	4
Staff attitude	6
Racecard and communication	3
Having a bet	7
Catering	8
Bars	6
Viewing and shelter	8
Total (out of 100)	**63**
Ranked joint 46th out of 59	
Hotels, pubs and restaurants ☆☆	

French Horn is open all day and, more important, serves its excellent food all day, too. Adnams and Marstons Pedigree adds to the appeal. In the centre of Southwell, a quiet and easily bypassed town, the historic Saracen's Head still holds court and remains a convenient place for an overnight stop.

● **TOP TIP:** French Horn at Upton.

STRATFORD

Winding up a telephone conversation with a senior racecourse executive, I mentioned that I would be spending the evening at Stratford. 'What are you going to see?' came the revealing response.

Stratford, honeypot to tourists and theatregoers, is simply not a racing town – even to racing people. This is a place of pageantry and postcards, of Shakespeare on the riverbank. Racing is an irrelevance, if not an irritant, to the predominant culture and the course reflects its status. It is featureless, almost as if striving to remain undetected from the cavalcade of open-top tour buses.

Logistically blessed, and with an apparently captive audience of year-round holidaymakers, Stratford should do itself rather well. Certainly, it has the potential to rank among the foremost country tracks, yet palpably it does not. Where Uttoxeter and Market Rasen forge enterprisingly ahead, Stratford seems bashful and unambitious. It chugs along respectably with an average crowd just above 4,000, but considering the setting and its enviable fixture list, based around summer weekends, this is unexceptional.

Possibly, the management is hamstrung by restrictions. The town bypass road made the course more accessible, yet the chance of an extra approach road has been blocked and traffic must enter down a narrow lane. At rush hour on Fridays, tailbacks are severe.

Springtime Friday nights are a tradition here. Until 1999, they staged the finale of the jump season and, in Mays gone by, jockeys and trainers of cavalier inclination would set up camp in the dingy cellar bar beneath the old stand.

All that has gone now and, from Stratford's viewpoint, its modern replacement is of dubious merit. A glass-fronted grandstand, opened in 1997 was conceivably designed by someone who had never been racing. That, at least, would explain the complete absence of cover over the members' terracing and the lack of elevation that contrives to obscure parts of even this intimate track.

CATERING

Perhaps the idea was to make everyone watch behind glass. There is an admirable view of racing from the champagne bar, for instance, but space is as limited as air. On a hot afternoon – and this, let's not forget, is a summer course – who would want to swelter the day away in there? Thankfully, airconditioning has now been installed.

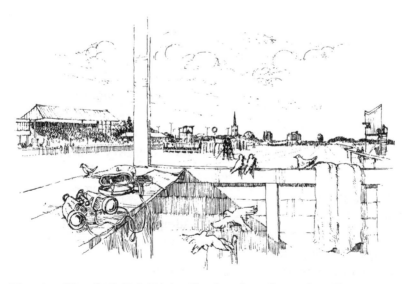

The spire of Stratford's Holy Trinity Church makes a feature from Shottery Meadow racecourse.

At a course where catering is unimaginative, this bar – selling plates of prawns or smoked salmon along with house champagne at a reasonable £26 – still wins out comfortably over the main restaurant, a tired room with a menu that might have remained unaltered since 1966.

Beef or sausage baps can be bought at the bars and, down the course, amid a hotchpotch of ugly buildings, the seafood shack, serving from a table evocative of a village fête, is a decent accompaniment to observing action from the last fence.

Stratford does some things well. Its **car parks** have improved in surface and organisation. Its **racecard**, now with glossy cover and editorial content, is good value, and the course

presentation has been stepped up with winner's enclosure interviews on the public address.

The betting ring is lively and there are more bookmakers in centre course, where families gather for picnics. They have to avert the eyes, though, from some wooden shacks that should have been replaced years ago, just like the smoky, depressing bar near the main entrance. That is the thing about Stratford. It is unattractive, almost to the point of ugliness, which is perhaps why the town seems to keep it at arm's length.

TRACK DETAILS

Stratford is flat, triangular in shape, and has a left-handed circuit of 1.25 miles. There are eight fences per circuit.

HOW TO GET THERE

By road: The racecourse lies 1 mile south-west of the town on the A439 Evesham road.
By rail: To Stratford-upon-Avon, then 1 mile by taxi.
Admission: Club stand £15, Tattersalls £11, course £5.

Website: www.stratfordracecourse.net

HOTELS, PUBS AND RESTAURANTS

The high mark of four stars does not reflect the pubs and restaurants in the town itself, for quantity greatly outweighs quality here. Stratford is a classic example of a tourist town 'dumbing down' its eating outlets to its perceived market and finding, at the end of it, that it has very few places that are not instantly forgettable. There are some improved wine bars in the main streets and Russon's, at the racecourse end of town, has a nice feel and good food. Desports is another good addition to the generally downmarket dining. You do not need to journey far outside town, though, for some very good pub food and attractive hotels. Stay at Billesley Manor, in a charming village on the Alcester side of the racecourse, or at the canalside Victoria Spa Lodge, a listed building in Bishopton Lane. Then seek out either the dependable Bell at Alderminster or the Fox and Goose at Armscote, where a recent change of owners – and name – has wrought some stylish improvements in food and décor.

• **TOP TIP**: Fox and Goose, Armscote.

MARKS OUT OF TEN

Access	5
Car parking	7
Comfort and cleanliness	6
Scenery and surroundings	5
Staff attitude	6
Racecard and communication	8
Having a bet	7
Catering	5
Bars	6
Viewing and shelter	5

Total (out of 100) 60
Ranked joint 53rd out of 59

Hotels, pubs and restaurants
☆☆☆☆

TAUNTON

Some courses have it made; others need to be enterprising. Taunton, where racing began in 1799, starts with the advantage of its site, on the edge of an atmospheric market town and overlooked by the Blackdown Hills, and the unquestioning patronage of those who keep farms and horses for miles around. Then it hits trouble.

A précis of its problems would include the country lane that provides

its only access, the car parks in a farm field and the fact that the charming view from the stands is often exclusive of racehorses as they disappear behind buildings or into the dip in the straight between the third and second-last fences.

Once, Taunton seemed content to wallow in the excuses of the backwater tracks. Thankfully, the present management is more positive. They can do little about the viewing but they have addressed other inadequacies and the place is now neater and more welcoming. Not yet a model country course, but definitely on the up.

There could be no better address for a rural racecourse than Orchard Portman, and rural it certainly is. The approach road, signposted through a warren of housing estates from the M5, could not cope with the traffic for the Christmas meeting but, despite weeks of rain, the ample **car park** area was not essential wellington boots

Taunton's circuit from the back section with the Blackdown Hills in the distance.

*Racing here started in 1877 and
they are still jumping today.*

territory. The laying of hard-standing tracks has been money well spent.

Staff at Taunton are amiable but ageing and some were overwhelmed by the size of the crowd. Entry, at a reasonable £12 for a day member's badge, was anything but slick. No queue for **racecards** but it was easy to see why – runners and form clear enough but spectators are entitled to expect an effort at editorial, or at least a guide to facilities, these days.

CATERING

Midwinter racing with its early starts, disorientates those who like to take lunch beforehand but the Orchard Restaurant, in a stand only ten years old, has a few window tables overlooking the course; pay £39 a head, eat three courses and stay all day. Down in the basement Saddle Room, those queueing for dry-looking fish and chips or chicken korma must have been desperate.

The Winning Post scored well for generous pork baps (£2.20) and having four pots of filter coffee on the go – pity about the plastic cups. The older Portman Stand serves even better coffee, and in mugs, in a friendly first-floor buffet with a picture window but the catering does lack originality – nothing home-made.

Time for a bet and, here, Taunton have set high standards. The layout of the betting ring is exemplary – it is close to the newly designed parade ring and large, with room to move. There are 32 bookmakers pitched here, another 18 in the hinterland of centre course still beloved of many, and a real relic in a shack with dust-encrusted lights and a sign introducing local bookmaker Peter Joliffe – '10p minimum stake'. A bargain at last.

Back a winner and head for the bars. Plenty of outlets, some with decent efforts at comfortable seating, but none is very appealing in the crush. Taunton provides a cosy owners' and trainers' bar but the public must choose either the Paddock Bar, which resembles an air-raid shelter, or the Winning Post. Either way, with no draught bitter the Blackthorn cider is favourite.

Return to the stands, frustrated, and peer at the

novice-chase runners now obscured by the additional natural hazard of the setting sun. With the hills and the beech trees and the old estate church to look at, though, even a loser has its compensations. And Taunton does have some excellent pubs.

HOTELS, PUBS AND RESTAURANTS

It is a sizeable provincial town now but there is still a nice, slightly old-fashioned feel to Taunton that makes it a favourite venue for both cricket and racing folk. The Castle Hotel is a landmark and its pampering style remains appealing. The main restaurant has always struck me as stuffy and pretentious, even when the food is exemplary, but it has also made a significant acknowledgement to changed times with its adjoining brasserie, Brazz. There are plenty of other hotels, of all sizes and style, worth considering, among them the Mount Somerset, a grand

TRACK DETAILS

The right-handed course is a long oval, about 1.25 miles round, and has seven fences in a complete circuit.

HOW TO GET THERE

By road: M5 (J25), then 2 miles south of the town on the B3170.
By rail: The course is 2.5 miles from Taunton station.
Admission: Members £12, paddock £10, course £5.

Website:
www.tauntonracecourse.co.uk

Regency mansion in Henlade, and the charming old Farthings at Hatch Beauchamp. These surrounding villages, evocatively named, also offer some fine country pubs, such as the Rising Sun at Knapp and the Rose and Crown at Stoke St Gregory. North of the town, on the A38 towards Bridgwater, the Walnut Tree at North Petherton is a very

MARKS OUT OF TEN

Access 6
Car parking 7
Comfort and cleanliness 7
Scenery and surroundings ... 8
Staff attitude 6
Racecard and communication 4
Having a bet 8
Catering 7
Bars 5
Viewing and shelter 5

Total (out of 100) 63
Ranked joint 46th out of 59

Hotels, pubs and restaurants
☆☆☆

good roadside hotel with some spacious rooms, a pubby bar and a civilised menu.

• **TOP TIP:** The village pubs.

THIRSK

It is amazing how many of the best ideas arise with the aid of agreeable refreshment in a cosy hostelry, and my research indicates that the creation of racecourses is no exception. Thirsk, for instance, owes its course to a lively discussion in the Golden Fleece Hotel, where a landowner named Frederick Bell decided that he had to have somewhere to run his own horses against those of his pals and it might as well be on the family estate.

As that was almost 150 years ago, it is not surprising that the place has changed a little. The Golden Fleece still dominates the cobbled

The parade ring at Thirsk.

square, a few yards down the road, but this market town course was largely rebuilt in the 1920s. It has not sacrificed its identity, though, and remains a clubby, locals' venue with a distinctive feel of rural Yorkshire.

CATERING

Still bibulous after all these years, too. This is among the best areas in Britain for pubs and many of them seem to have an affinity with racing. In nearby Masham, an independent brewery produces the estimable Black Sheep bitter and Thirsk wins high marks for serving it on handpump in its Tattersalls bar – a lesson for the majority who lean lazily on tasteless Australian lagers and keg bitters.

I discovered the Black Sheep in an anonymous building called, forbiddingly, Grimthorpe Hall. Although I entered with heavy heart, it was a pleasant surprise to discover a long room lightened by ceiling windows and hanging baskets. There were carpets on the floor and tables to sit at, which may sound elementary but is a good deal more than is found in comparable bars else-where. Football has learnt that people treated like stray animals will generally behave like them; enlightenment is spreading slowly to racing.

Thirsk is not a snobs' course but it does set certain standards, applying a dress code in its members' area – though I saw some creative variations on the compulsory collar and tie – and charging a steepish £14 entry. There is a whiff of old money about, especially in the Hambleton Rooms. These stand at the rear of the main stand, its red brick softened by trained

TRACK DETAILS

A left-handed, oval track just over 1.25 miles in extent with a run-in of half a mile. It is relatively flat, but on the sharp side.

creeper, and comprise a poorly sited restaurant – too small, too narrow and no view of anything relevant – and a snug bar with decent wines and Pimm's by the glass. It is, though, a little like intruding on a remote village local, where the assembled company has been unchanged for years.

Things are more modern in the smart Manton suite, which has a civilised bar and buffet and some corporate areas, but this is a dislocated facility without a view. Much the best area on the course is on the first floor of the club stand, where bars occupy adjoining rooms looking down on the finishing line. Farther along the stand, a block of bench seats offers a sedentary view of a course so flat and narrow that the runners never stray from sight.

This is a neat course, not unlike its neighbour, Ripon, though not quite as pretty. The paddock has only one tall tree here, compared with several at Ripon, and the weighing-room is a strangely ugly structure. There is a pastoral outlook, the centre

HOW TO GET THERE

By road: Off the A61, which connects directly with the A1 and A19.
By rail: Thirsk station is 10 minutes walk from the course.
Admission: Members £15, Tattersalls £10, family ring £3.

Website: www.thirskracecourse.net

course occupied only by a cricket ground and a cornfield.

No complaints about access – it is easily found off a variety of trunk roads and flagged by excellent signposts – nor **car parking**, which is mainly across the road from the main entrance. The **racecard**, though, is featureless, lacking in content and imagination.

Staff here are dressed in green overall coats of the type worn by Ronnie Barker in *Open All Hours*. Some even look the part, a shade too lugubrious for the good of the place.

Bookmakers would have reason for similar expressions as

they balance on the sharp descent from the main stand – gratifyingly, on the back foot even before battle commences.

HOTELS, PUBS AND RESTAURANTS

Any trip to Thirsk is to be eagerly anticipated if only for the proximity of the Crab and Lobster at Asenby, which contrives to be all things to all men – atmospheric pub, brilliant restaurant and luxurious if quirky hotel. If only there were more places like this on the landscape. It is set just off the A168, barely four miles from the course, and stands out like a beacon even in an area enviably served for pubs and hotels. Crab Manor, the elegant hotel part, has rooms themed on exotic holiday destinations, lovely lounges and a tennis court in the gardens. The pub, with four real ales, a fabulous blackboard menu and a top wine list, is alongside. Thirsk itself has the Golden Fleece Hotel, an old haunt of Dick Turpin, in the

MARKS OUT OF TEN	
Access	7
Car parking	7
Comfort and cleanliness	7
Scenery and surroundings	7
Staff attitude	6
Racecard and communication	5
Having a bet	6
Catering	6
Bars	8
Viewing and shelter	7
Total (out of 100)	**66**

Ranked 43rd out of 59

Hotels, pubs and restaurants
☆ ☆ ☆ ☆

marketplace, while Sheppards in nearby Sowerby is a pretty restaurant with rooms. Two other pubs worth looking up are the Nag's Head near the A1 at Pickhill, where the food is good and the landlord, Edward Baynton, is a fervent racing man, and the Wombwell Arms at Wass, near Ampleforth.

- **TOP TIP**: The Crab and Lobster.

TOWCESTER

Not so long ago, habitués of rural racecourses required the constitution and equipment of intrepid hikers. Patience and tolerance were essential, along with maps and waterproof clothing. You could not survive without a wry sense of humour and it was as well to possess an undemanding palate.

Such accessories remain sensible precautions in certain primitive spots, as this whistle-stop odyssey has discovered, but the revolution now has an irresistible momentum. There are courses which have taken such enlightened strides with their appearance and attitude that anyone revisiting after an absence of, say, three years, would find them barely recognisable. Nowhere exemplifies this progress better, or more subtly, than Towcester.

It was always a striking venue, a country estate racecourse with a splendid stone gateway and a natural panorama of middle England. A course for staunch jumping folk, solidly tweedy, thriving on ambience rather than appointments. For a time, though, it hovered in that grey area between charm and decay

The entrance screen at Towcester was the work of William Croggan in 1822.

and the many who cared for it were entitled to fear for its future.

Fret no more. In the brave new racecourse world of enterprise, those that demonstrate their worth are well rewarded and Towcester is self-evidently flourishing. Along with the timeless setting there is now a sense of vitality, almost a commercial cuteness. There are smart green signs, companies entertaining in strategically placed marquees, a sequence of advertising boards along the rail on the run-in – and it has not spoiled the old place one bit.

Towcester is a catalogue of choices. Pronunciation, for instance. Should it sound like the breakfast bread grill or a pet pig? There seems no strong consensus. Then there is the matter of approach roads, for this is a country track wedged conveniently between the M1 and M40, with the A5 directly alongside. Signposts are spread so generously that it is hard, even for the geographically challenged, to get lost.

The working-day for boxers is typical of the secondary events that have been running at Towcester.

The greatest of choices, though, is between ancient and modern. Previously, Towcester only did old, and did it to a fund of goodwill from regulars who loved the steamy windows and stained floors of the bars and the queue to climb the steps to the top deck of the 1928 stand, with its wonderfully complete views. I know. I loved it all with them. But it could not go on because, alone, it was not enough.

Now, the ancient stand must be replaced, for safety reasons.

HOW TO GET THERE

By road: Via the M1 (J15A) and then the A43. The A5 also bypasses the course.

By rail: To Northampton or Milton Keynes; a bus service runs to the course from both town centres.

Admission: Members £14, Tattersalls £10, course £6.

Website: www.towcester-racecourse.co.uk

CATERING

The old stand bar – with views to parade ring from one window and course from the other – is decorated in conservatory style, with wicker chairs. Down the course, though, the Grace Stand, 70 years newer than its venerable partner, provides the comforts and amenities appropriate to a new generation.

It could be better still. The splendid first floor of the Grace Stand should be a public viewing restaurant rather than being given over to corporate guests. The catering still needs improvement, too. There is room for no more than 20 in the wooden hut – like a village cricket pavilion – that houses the feature seafood bar and other eating choices are bland.

The winner's enclosure remains inadequate and would be better moved into the parade ring. The **car parks**, though vast and well accessed, are set on variable surfaces – avoid the grass, which is prone to become a bog in midwinter.

This is an addictive place, from the secluded lunchtime pubs in surrounding villages to the rickety old number board in centre course, as much a part of the deal as the sight of Hugo Bevan – clerk of the course for 20 years – chain-smoking his way through another anxious meeting. Bevan entered retirement recently, knowing his beloved Towcester is in good hands.

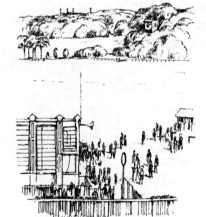

From Towcester's now condemned stand the house and church of Easton Neston can be seen among the trees.

TRACK DETAILS

A right-handed course with ten fences per circuit. Stamina is at a premium because of the steep climb to the home turn and uphill finish.

HOTELS, PUBS AND RESTAURANTS

Some interesting and atmospheric spots to eat and drink around here, though a shortage of decent hotels without venturing into the formularised and corporate markets of Northampton or Milton Keynes. The exception is Vine House, an 18th-century cottage in the neighbouring village of Paulerspury (two miles south on the A5) which has nine letting rooms and a good restaurant. You can eat well at two places approaching Towcester from junction 15 of the M1 – the Roade House at Roade and Bruerne's Lock in the canalside village of Stoke Bruerne, where the Boat pub is also recommended. The Greyhound at Milton Malsor, in a similar area just off the A508, has 20 wines by the glass, while a very charming pub in the locality is the King's Arms at Farthingstone, south of Daventry, where the real ales and the flagstoned, fireside bar are the attractions.

● **TOP TIP**: King's Arms, Farthingstone.

MARKS OUT OF TEN

Access 8
Car parking 6
Comfort and cleanliness 8
Scenery and surroundings ... 8
Staff attitude 7
Racecard and
communication 9
Having a bet 7
Catering 6
Bars 7
Viewing and shelter 8

Total (out of 100) 74
Ranked joint 12th out of 59

Hotels, pubs and restaurants
☆☆☆

213

UTTOXETER

Not so long ago, a reference to Uttoxeter was likely to bring one of two reactions – indifference or ignorance. Many people would have been unable to find the place on a map and those who had done so were probably in no rush to return. And yet, within a few years of energetic enhancement, the racecourse has raised the profile of an unexceptional Staffordshire town. For devotees of rural jump racing, this is a mecca.

If it is possible for a course to perform too well for its own good, Uttoxeter is doing so. On high days and holidays, which make up a fair proportion of the fixtures here, it is like Cheltenham in miniature, daunting queues snaking away from each and every facility. Like a sprouting teenager, Uttoxeter is bursting out of its clothing.

Better that, though, than the decay and apathy of old. Uttoxeter has been voted 'best regional racecourse' for seven of the past eight years and it shows few signs of wanting to give somewhere else a chance. Every visit reveals a new improvement.

Its average crowds are bigger than those at Kempton Park, Haydock and Newbury. Its appeal is an atmosphere that still owes something to the country fair, yet now with the slickness and appointments demanded by the modern spectator. Few racecourses offer more enjoyment per square foot.

That said, certain health warnings apply. On Midlands National day, and again on Easter Monday, those who leave their arrival late will find the tailback extending around the town. They will also find the **car parks** stretched, if not full. Blood pressure sufferers must beware.

Finding the place is no longer a problem. The A50 dual-carriage-way link between the M6 and M1 passes its gates. Signposts are plentiful, too, and those who arrive flustered and late will find well-trained staff in green blazers and badges to soothe them.

The **racecard** has crept up in price to £1.50 but this can be justified when it includes editorial, a plan of facilities and, usually, jockeys' silks in colour. The ubiquitous Stan Clarke owns Uttoxeter and he knows how to put on a show. His redesigned parade ring – still short of spectator room and constantly packed – is host to a series of interviews with jockeys and trainers.

Band music and green and white paint identify every Clarke course but this is his flagship and he remains a hands-on chairman, mingling with a prominent name badge and fielding any brickbats with the attention of one who genuinely cares.

The parade ring at Uttoxeter, and beyond it the railway station and church.   **215**

CATERING

Most of the achievements here are a masterful camouflage of buildings that could otherwise depress as the aged shacks they really are. One, not much bigger than a garden shed, buzzes with the happy chatter of diners and drinkers in its metamorphosis as Hoops, a champagne bar and seafood eatery.

Another, way down the course near the spectacle of the final fence, is the John Kenny Bar. This is the cheap quarter, where facilities are shamefully neglected by so many tracks, yet here there is a log fire, posters on the walls, comfortable chairs and fresh coffee. And, yes, the usual notice from the chairman asking for any complaints to be addressed to him personally.

Upstairs in the main stand, there is a members' 'platinum area' which disappoints – not least in charging £2.50 for a glass of wine out of a box. Uttoxeter usually corrects its errors quickly. A coffee shop, hopelessly disorganised on one visit, had been significantly revamped a month later.

Betting is not a joy at Uttoxeter – the ring is too shallow and crowded for that – and comfort levels are inevitably modest

TRACK DETAILS

The course is an oval of approximately 1.25 miles. There are eight fences per circuit with a run-in of 170 yards.

HOW TO GET THERE

By road: The course is half a mile south-east of the town centre off the B5017, which can be reached via the M6 (J15), M1 (J23A) or M42 (J10) and then the A50 or A518.
By rail: Uttoxeter station is adjacent to the course.
Admission: Members £15, Tattersalls £11, centre course enclosure £5.

Website: www.uttoxeterracecourse.co.uk

when the place is bulging with crowds of 15,000. Go on a quieter day; the racing will still be decent and there will be time to savour the agricultural views and the ambience of perhaps the most progressive course in the land.

HOTELS, PUBS AND RESTAURANTS

There is some excellent beer in the area, courtesy of the Marston's brewery, but for good pubs to drink it in it is best to head south from Uttoxeter to Abbots Bromley (the Crown) or Tutbury, where the timbered Olde Dog and Partridge has some bedrooms and a busy carvery as bonuses. Not much to commend Uttoxeter itself, but the Derbyshire Dales are only a few miles to the north and Callow Hall, in Ashbourne, is a charming hotel for a Friday night stop before one of the hectic Uttoxeter Saturdays. Only a couple of miles east of the course, Beeches at Waldley, near

MARKS OUT OF TEN

Access	9
Car parking	7
Comfort and cleanliness	5
Scenery and surroundings	8
Staff attitude	9
Racecard and communication	9
Having a bet	5
Catering	7
Bars	8
Viewing and shelter	7

Total (out of 100) 74
Ranked joint 12th out of 59

Hotels, pubs and restaurants
☆ ☆

Doveridge, is an example to all of what farmers can do when agriculture becomes uneconomic. The owners began with bed and breakfast on their dairy farm but Beeches has grown in style and stature to the point where it is now a ten-room hotel with a very good restaurant.

● **TOP TIP:** Beeches at Waldley.

217

WARWICK

It was a heavy-hearted drive to Warwick – not because this has ever been a hard course to reach but rather a hard course to love. Boggy car parks, soggy catering, squalid amenities and inadequate vantage points had long since soured me against the place. For all the talk of a new stand, I doubted that much had changed.

I was wrong. A great deal has been improved within this ancient, idiosyncratic track. It still has an air of melancholy in its structures and outlook, for it must remain an indelibly urban racecourse, not

---

Warwick home straight, with the town and its tower of St Mary's Church dominating the hill.

a thing of beauty. However, the prolific and reliable nature of the racing – meetings every month of the year – is now matched by the environment.

The first surprise is that the 'new' stand is not new at all. From a distance – and most things are viewed that way on this strangely straggling course – it looks unchanged. It is a listed building, which made the Edwardian ironwork inviolate and the planned conversion fraught, but inside it is a triumph of pragmatic design.

Bars and catering outlets are sprinkled thoughtfully, and there is a functional ground floor where betting and drinking co-exist instructively. Too many rooms – including the advertised Kingmaker Restaurant – were given over to private or corporate parties but this was at least the mark of a thriving venue.

Nothing is luxurious, for this is not that kind of racecourse, but it would be churlish to quibble with a facility that is clean, neat and well ordered. The most welcome change has brought capacious steppings

Warwick's winners' enclosure features the county emblem.

on the first floor, open at the ends but protected by an extended roof, transforming the viewing facilities from the confined terrace of old.

Even now, it is impossible to follow the runners all around Warwick. They disappear for a stretch behind a hill, where legend insists that all manner of shady practices preceded the deterrent of mobile cameras. The long back straight, though, is a steeplechasing spectacle and the fact that it can now be watched in comfort is sufficient reason to revise previous prejudices about Warwick.

Of course, it still has its irritations. Though minutes from the M40, it is accessed through tight residential streets, where more signs would be useful. The official **car park**, just past the diverting head-quarters of the Warwick Girls' Marching Band, is a field, often water-logged, and the main public car park is narrow and inefficient.

These are the millstones of a town course. The centre of Warwick squats immediately behind the stand and the panorama from the new terrace is of second-city suburbia. Perhaps the next project should be to obliterate the centre-course stand, which is ugly.

Back, though, to the plus points. The **racecard** is distinctive and informative, supplemented by gossipy interviews in the winner's enclosure. Smart signs guide the stranger around the concourses and there are gestures of care in the flowerbeds and benches.

CATERING

At the business end of the course – as opposed to the betting and viewing end, which is a fair hike towards Coventry – the Paddock Suite, though largely corporate, contains a fine ground-floor bar and bistro. This is one of several venues for lunch, though tables do need booking.

There is a cosy seafood bar with an admirable wine list and an informal soup cellar for those who want a snack on the run. In the new stand, the rooms are named after appropriate racecourse luminaries. The

There is interest even in odd corners on racecourses, and Warwick is no exception.

Duke's Room, celebrating David Nicholson, contained a noisy private party. Typical.

Good hot food, such as lamb casserole and poached salmon, is served cheerfully in the members' bar, where mugs of decent coffee at £1 are another welcome feature. Bitter and lager sell at a reasonable £2.20 per pint and one-third bottles of French wine are £3.30. The betting ring here is well sited and atmospheric. Now, though, there are alternative reasons for coming.

HOW TO GET THERE

By road: The course is situated 2 miles from the M40 (J15). It is west of the town on the A41.
By rail: Warwick station, then taxi or 15 minutes walk.
Admission: Club £15, Tattersalls £11, course £5.

Website:
www.warwickracecourse.co.uk

HOTELS, PUBS AND RESTAURANTS

The M40 has brought business traffic to Warwick, and with it some large hotels. On the Longbridge roundabout, a mile down the road from the racecourse, Hilton and Holiday Inn both have outlets but those who prefer something more individual will take the Cirencester road (A429) to Barford where the Glebe Hotel, a former rectory, has comfortable rooms and good leisure facilities in an attractive setting. Ardencote Manor at Claverdon, towards Henley-in-Arden, has a golf course on site, and the village also boasts the busy Red Lion pub. The grandest hotel around is Mallory Court at Bishop's Tachbrook. Pubs are not great, hereabouts, but the Rose and Crown in Warwick's marketplace has a handsome bar and good real ale. Leamington has a fair choice of restaurants, including a decent Chinese in Emperors, and Simpsons at Kenilworth is a very popular neighbourhood bistro.

- **TOP TIP**: Claverdon for pub, hotel and golf.

TRACK DETAILS

The flat-racing course is oval in shape and 1.25 miles in distance. It favours sharp, nippy horses. The jumps course is spacious and rises at the finish, putting a premium on stamina. Both tracks are left-handed.

MARKS OUT OF TEN

Access	7
Car parking	4
Comfort and cleanliness	8
Scenery and surroundings	5
Staff attitude	7
Racecard and communication	7
Having a bet	9
Catering	9
Bars	8
Viewing and shelter	8

Total (out of 100) 72
Ranked joint 17th out of 59

Hotels, pubs and restaurants
☆☆

WETHERBY

Creating an ideal racecourse is not an exact science. Location is critical; amenities, attitude and standard of racing are all essential parts of the jigsaw. Wetherby meets each of these criteria but it has something else besides – the intangible bonus, denied to so many, of a memorable atmosphere.

Even on a quiet midwinter day when the runners are few and the crowd modest, Wetherby is a stimulating place to be, a purveyor of all that is good in National Hunt racing. It sustained this mood through years when its facilities were gently decaying and it still casts

Beyond the racecourse buildings stands Ingmanthorpe Hall, typifying the long association of squire and horse-racing.

223

its spell now that it offers one of the glitziest grandstands in the racing land.

Layout is the key. Wetherby lacks for little, these days, but it remains a course where everything happens in close-up. The stands seem to be right on top of the racing, the line of fences up the home straight a stirring sight, while the paddock, winner's enclosure and saddling area, directly behind, now form a theatrical feature.

The recent developments dazzle like futuristic airport terminals but the trick has been to implant them among their ancient, adored but increasingly impractical predecessors without loss of character. So far this has been accomplished skilfully, but Wetherby's upgrading is incomplete and some sensitive decisions still await.

The most obvious of Wetherby's attributes is setting. The A1 rumbles past the home turn, providing an ease of access second to none, yet the surroundings are rural and appealing. More signposts are needed in Wetherby itself but the course now has two entry roads, from front and rear, and an overdue improvement in the organisation of the **car park**. This is free and vast but much of it lies on undulating ground, subject to winter waterlogging. Tractors may be required for towing purposes.

On my first visit to Wetherby, some years ago, I had a dispute with the car-park attendant and a mix-up over badges on which the gate staff were implacably unhelpful. I entered the course seething but it still seduced me with its ambience and persuaded me back, time and again. Over the years, the staff attitude has become notably sunnier, their numbers now augmented by the smartly uniformed team supervising the Millennium Stand.

For some reason, this racing landmark was opened by Richard Whiteley, who apparently presents a television game show. That apart, it has a lot going for it. It is one thing being stylish and modern but quite another producing customer-friendly facilities. Wetherby has largely succeeded, principally in creating excellent vantage points and a tier of unusually comfortable seats.

CATERING

The plush stairways feel sterile on the quieter days and imaginative racing art would help. The main third-floor restaurant also faces back, to the paddock, rather than forward to the racing but this enables a premium price (£60 plus) to be charged for the dine-and-view rooms, with their own private balconies.

The public buffet is small and poorly sited, tucked into a corner next to kitchen and toilet doors, but as the caterers here are those northern racecourse regulars, Craven Gilpin, the food is dependably hearty – lasagnes, cottage pies and giant sausage and mushroom baguettes.

Bars are startlingly diverse, from the plush Marston Moor, with its lengthy champagne list, to the A1 Bar down the course, in a faded conservatory building with wooden floors that has a certain charm, despite the familiar beer monopoly of Yorkshire keg bitter and Australian lager.

The old members' stand is dwarfed and partly disused nowadays but still offers the best

TRACK DETAILS

Left-handed with easy turns. It provides a fair test for any horse. There are nine fences. The slightly uphill run-in is relatively short for the chasers.

views of racing from its top-floor gallery, limited in space and well worth the extra £1 to climb the old staircase. The 100 seats are usually protected fiercely by earlycomers but there is space for 250 to stand and many stay for the duration, gazing across the pastoral scenes towards Harrogate and wondering, perhaps, whether the winnings should be spent in the Malt Shovel at Brearton.

HOTELS, PUBS AND RESTAURANTS

Yorkshire is a county of such contrasts and it is hard to believe that this area is only a short drive up the A1 from Pontefract and Doncaster. Good

HOW TO GET THERE

By road: East of town, off the B1224 York road.
By rail: Leeds station is 12 miles away, then bus or taxi to Wetherby.
Admission: Club £16–£17.50, Tattersalls £10–£11 (prices vary depending on meeting), course £3.

Website: www.wetherbyracing.co.uk

MARKS OUT OF TEN

Access 9
Car parking 7
Comfort and cleanliness 8
Scenery and surroundings ... 7
Staff attitude 7
Racecard and communication 7
Having a bet 7
Catering 8
Bars 6
Viewing and shelter 9

Total (out of 100) 75
Ranked 11th out of 59

Hotels, pubs and restaurants
☆ ☆ ☆

hotels abound, from the opulent Wood Hall, which stands overlooking the course, to the more personal Linton Springs in Linton, where the rooms are large, the restaurant snug and the garden contains a private golf range. Harrogate, with its broad sweep of the hotel market, is only a short drive away and also offers such restaurants as the Drum and Monkey (for fish) and Olivers. At Ferrensby, north of Wetherby and only just off the A1, the General Tarleton is a smart coaching inn with good rooms and a courtyard restaurant. Personal recommendations from the host of surrounding pubs must include the Harewood Arms in Michael Dickinson country (also a good overnight stop-off) and the Star and Garter in the lovely village of Kirkby Overblow.

● **TOP TIP**: Linton Springs Hotel.

WINCANTON

You can tell a lot about a racecourse by its bars. They don't all need to be plush or modern – indeed, many courses would suffer for such sanitising – but to perform their function as the migrating grounds for every level of racing society they must be comfortable, atmospheric and well stocked. The best in the country are to be found at Wincanton.

Every regular racegoer knows that there is a particular ambience present in a bar shortly before the first, as racecards are perused, anecdotes exchanged and predictions pronounced. The magic of the moment is irreparably dimmed, though, if the furnishings are

decrepit, the staff offhand, the wine sour and the whisky extortionate.

It happens too often, even at a time when most courses have recognised that they are judged by such matters. Too many still take the lazy option, both in the bland, unappealing design of their bars and the unimaginative stock. What a pleasure, then, to report on a course that has made sensitive improvements in every area.

The rolling Somerset countryside can be enjoyed from Wincanton's stands.

The racecard and communication at Wincanton are surpassed only by its fantastic bars.

Wincanton always had a certain spartan charm but its bars are now civilised by carpets and better décor; they are also sufficiently ample to be comfortable, even on the high-profile days.

From an ancient timber and corrugated-iron structure, magnetically cosy inside, to the smartly functional Tattersalls bar with course literature and magazines in its entrance lobby, all show signs of care and style. Just as important is the booze on sale, including decent wines at only £1.85 a glass and Badger Tanglefoot bitter on handpump. There is more than one reason for finding someone else to drive here.

Wincanton is in deepest Somerset, hidden among disorientatingly winding country lanes. Though close to the A303 trunk road, it is not an easy place to access and it can be still harder to get away.

The **car park** is a massive field where many are blocked in by the late, arrogant or ignorant and from where all are decanted on to a road that was designed for a couple of farm tractors a day. Only Bangor and Hexham can match Wincanton's sense of being in the middle of nowhere.

This, of course, can also be a virtue. Looking out across the farms and hills from the Wincanton stands, there is scarcely any habitation to blight the view. The surrounding villages are lovely, their greens, churches and pubs the stuff of chocolate-box photography.

Wincanton is more than just a pretty face, though. Its racing is of higher quality than most comparable tracks and its infrastructure has advanced, without betraying the clubby, country feel that is vital to the attraction of courses such as this and fellow charmers like Ludlow and Kelso.

Entrances have been smartened up considerably. New brown signs direct spectators around the course. There is a crèche and play area for children, while investment in fresh paint and new furnishings takes nothing away from the nostalgia of the honours boards in the oldest bar.

The Hatherleigh Stand, built in 1990, offers tiered seating behind the picture windows of its top floor – fabulous views across a course where the one obstruction is a listed farm building. A 1960s' stand is less impressive, not least for being built at the wrong angle and elevation.

Wincanton's **racecard**, at least for the bigger days, is printed with full colours and another welcome development is the public address interviews conducted from a cramped and inadequate winners' enclosure that would surely be better integrated with the paddock.

CATERING

The catering is almost as impressive as the bars, though it is a shame that the airy Kingwell Restaurant is set back behind the main stands and thus offers only a glimpse of the action from its tables.

The Tattersalls buffet serves chicken curry or sausage and mash, each at £4, but the best atmosphere lies within the recently converted annexe of the oldest bar, where fish pie can be followed by home-made cakes. Everything you could wish from a rural racecourse.

HOW TO GET THERE

By road: North of the town on the B3081, just off the A303 bypass.

By rail: To Templecombe (courtesy transport to course), Castle Cary or Gillingham, then bus or taxi journey.

Admission: Members £15, Tattersalls £10, course £5.

Website:
www.wincantonracecourse.co.uk

MARKS OUT OF TEN

Access 5
Car parking 5
Comfort and cleanliness 8
Scenery and surroundings ... 9
Staff attitude 7
Racecard and
communication 9
Having a bet 6
Catering 8
Bars 10
Viewing and shelter 7

Total (out of 100) **74**
Ranked joint 12th out of 59

Hotels, pubs and restaurants
☆☆☆☆

TRACK DETAILS

A sharp, right-handed, oval
track of about 1.5 miles.

HOTELS, PUBS AND RESTAURANTS

Despite being so close to the A303
dual carriageway, there is an air of
remote rurality to Wincanton that
lends itself to country house
hotels and village pubs. The area
does not disappoint and has three
hotels worthy of strong
recommendation – the George, a
coaching inn set in the
marketplace of nearby Castle
Cary; the Austrian-run but
quintessentially English Stock Hill
House at Gillingham on the way
to Shaftesbury; and Holbrook
House, a 15-room hotel in
Wincanton itself that is everything
you would expect from this locality. Truffles at Bruton is a good
dining option if you are staying
overnight (it only opens for
dinner) and a series of decent
pubs is headed by Hunters Lodge,
just off the A303 at the racecourse
exit and a hugely popular spot for
pre-race drinks and food. The Old
Smithy at Charlton Musgrave, a
mile from the course, is so quaint
it belongs in another age, while a
dozen miles back up the A303 the
village of Hindon offers two
stylish pubs with rooms, the
Grosvenor and the Lamb.

- **TOP TIP:** Holbrook House
  Hotel.

WINDSOR

Beneath the highest level, where quality of racing alone identifies all but the most inept, the successful courses are invariably those who achieve a niche market. There is no better example than Windsor, which plays shamelessly and skilfully upon its reputation as an antidote to the Monday night blues. Every Monday of summer, while daylight hours permit, upwards of 4,000 people leave offices and factories for a lazy, hazy evening on the banks of the Thames. The racing is never less than competitive, but it is the atmosphere of escapism which tempts so many regulars.

Briefly, I mourned the passing of jump racing at Windsor but it can now be assessed as a sound decision. It was never more than an idiosyncratic jumps track, anyway, and summer nights suit this place so

Windsor racecourse has stands dating back to the first meeting.

231

much better. It is a notable acquisition for the Arena portfolio and, in 2001, a long weekend of racing on a Saturday, Sunday and Monday in early June made good use of the venue.

Not everything about Windsor is welcoming. Though barely a mile from the M4, the rush-hour traffic can be one mighty deterrent. Signposting is adequate and police cones are helpful but access to the track itself is through a single gate and across quaint but frustrating wooden bridges. To arrive in character with the meeting, take the shuttle boat to the course from Windsor bridge. It has a bar on board and will save you the encumbrance of paying £2 for what can be haphazardly organised **parking**.

If stress levels are high on arrival, the environment is designed to soothe. Traditional gatemen are elderly, hatted and friendlier than they look. **Racecards** cost £2, nothing elaborate bar clarity and information with a simple map of facilities – replicated at points around the course – that is especially good in identifying the excellent facilities for the disabled.

Like its pricing structure, in which the excessive charge of £16 for a club badge is compensated by free admission up to 17 years old rather than the customary 16, Windsor is very much the curate's egg in its amenities.

The clubhouse is splendid, all polished mahogany, elegant stairways decorated with racing art, snug bars and the most luxurious loos in racing. Next door, the Tattersalls long room has grubby carpets and the air of having missed a spring clean, while the Cellar Bar that stands between the buildings is a revolting hovel of the type that still somehow survives on too many racecourses.

Dressing for the occasion has always been a feature of going to the races.

Shelter on the stands is inadequate – one more reason why this is a summer track – and the angle of the course, not to mention its figure-of-eight conformation, make viewing an unsatisfactory sequence of rear views and head-ons. Punting, though, is somehow more fun here, not only because the ring is well sited and invariably busy but for the sense of a day's work done that permeates the mood.

CATERING

There are two great social areas at Windsor. At the champagne bar on the lawn, you are highly likely to encounter Vinnie Jones and his entourage, filming commitments permitting, and if the bubbly does not suit mood or pocket you can drink reasonable wine at £3 a glass or fresh filter coffee. Seafood and Oriental stalls on the lawn are equally in demand.

Upstairs in the Royal Windsor Stand, the Castle Restaurant is justly popular for its slick catering, ambience and view of the racing. It is packed every Monday, testimony to the demand for a decent meal with a view, and no enterprising course, alert to modern requirements, can afford to be without such a restaurant.

A mile from Windsor Castle, with the river beguilingly alongside, Windsor could be among the most beautiful of our racecourses but it is not. Its flat functionality is exemplified by a weighing-room of red brick and blue paint that could be a suburban public library. Redeemed by

HOW TO GET THERE

By road: From the M4 (J6) or M3 (J3).
By rail: Windsor (Central) and Windsor and Eton (Riverside) are both 2 miles from the course.
Admission: Club £16, Tattersalls £11, Silver Ring £5.

Website:
www.windsor-racecourse.co.uk

MARKS OUT OF TEN

Access 7
Car parking 6
Comfort and cleanliness 7
Scenery and surroundings ... 7
Staff attitude 7
Racecard and
communication 7
Having a bet 8
Catering 8
Bars 8
Viewing and shelter 4

Total (out of 100) **69**
Ranked joint 33th out of 59

Hotels, pubs and restaurants
☆☆

TRACK DETAILS

A figure-of-eight circuit with a
right-hand turn leading into
a straight of 5 furlongs.

its trees, lawn and that delightful clubhouse, it still has a lot to recommend it.

HOTELS, PUBS AND RESTAURANTS

If anything, Windsor suffers still more than its neighbour, Ascot, from the syndrome of overpriced hotels and pubs, simply because it is a honeypot for the migration of American tourists with money to burn. Oakley Court and Sir Christopher Wren's House are fine hotels in the town but dauntingly expensive, a comment that also applies to the Castle, where room prices start at £150. Best, then, to turn your back on the tourist trappings and head up river towards Cookham, a nice village with two smart pubs – Bel and the Dragon and the Chequers, both with decent food. Closer to the course, the Belgian Arms on the attractive village green at Holyport and the Palmers Arms at Dorney are good alternatives. For fine dining, Bray is the place – the Waterside for the experience, the Fish Inn for the atmosphere – although the habit of closing on Mondays is a considerable drawback for a course doing most of its racing on Monday evenings.

• **TOP TIP**: Get out of town.

WOLVERHAMPTON

Racing at Wolverhampton began in 1887, but the date that really matters is 1962. It was then that this became the first course to stage a Saturday evening card, a prophetic event indeed. Nowadays Wolverhampton serves two purposes, one as a betting necessity and the other as a novel entertainment, racing's regular Saturday night out.

There were those of us who mourned when jump racing virtually disappeared from this venue, drab and dreary though it had been. We were wrong. The daring makeover to an all-weather flat track staging 56 meetings a year, 18 of them under floodlights, has unarguably worked.

Even the greatest of salesmen – and Arena Leisure, which owns the course and identified the market, is far from shy – could not promote Wolverhampton on quality alone. Most of the jockeys and horses are virtually unknown. The racing may be dire and the crowds among the smallest in the country but it does have an audience and, when the lights are on, an atmosphere.

Punters may go to Wolverhampton on a mid-week afternoon but Saturday nights draw a different, jollier mix, savouring the added blessing that racing in the dark does wonders for the Wolverhampton scenery.

Once, the racecourse was wedged into a depressed and degenerating estate. Now, sprightly new residences are springing up around the purpose-built access roads and the portentous entrance drive. Dunstall Park, which once hid itself away as if embarrassed, is now signposted around this labyrinthine town, a tourist attraction to rival the Black Country Museum.

The welcome experience here is excellent, for the **car park** – once a boggy field with a patrolling tractor – is now among the best in the country and the staff all know what they are doing, a pleasant variation on certain racecourses.

TRACK DETAILS

The all-weather flat-racing course is a left-handed oval, just under 1 mile round, with a fibresand surface.

You enter through what looks like the lobby of a hotel, and turns out to be just that. For £79 per room, you can forget the drive home and stay the night. Arena will soon be adding hotels to most of their courses – not merely for the benefit of weary punters but to help make the venues efficient year-round. Traditionalists may sniff but this is a business, not a rich man's hobby.

The **racecard** needs some attention and imagination but viewing of the tight track is excellent from the stands, where you will seldom be short of elbow room, and there is a lively market in the shallow betting ring.

The parade ring and stands before Wolverhampton's radical redevelopment.

CATERING

Bad weather is almost an irrelevance here. The Saturday night crowd does not venture outdoors much, if at all. Some wander the civilised concourse, with its fast-food outlets and its pub-style bars, but the real attraction is the restaurants – all five of them.

The members' restaurant is what you would expect on most courses but its sister establishments are way above the norm. Harry's, a simple bistro, is set in the hotel with windows overlooking the paddock; Ringside is a vast ground-floor room with a carvery menu and cinema screens to view the racing; Lesters is a neat 45-seater with head-on views down the straight.

Much the best reason for attending Wolverhampton, though, is its feature restaurant, Zongalero. It seats 400 at tables set on three tiers, each with a decent view of the track through the vast glass frontage. There is a welcome drink, a reasonable three-course meal, slickly served, and an adequate wine list. Televisions on the tables offer betting shows as well as the live racing and, with Tote staff circulating, it is not even necessary to move to place a bet. A band plays between races, and continues afterwards. Kids love it. At £32.90 a head, it is full every Saturday night, and deserves to be.

HOTELS, PUBS AND RESTAURANTS

There is a Holiday Inn on site here, which is not only a fine idea for a course concentrating its efforts on the Saturday night market but, quite possibly, a pointer to the way ahead for

HOW TO GET THERE

By road: Track is 1 mile north of town on the A449, accessible from the M54 (J2) and the M6 (J12).
By rail: Wolverhampton station (London Euston) is 1 mile from the course.
Admission: Members £15, Tattersalls £8.

Website: www.wolverhampton-racecourse.co.uk

MARKS OUT OF TEN

Access	8
Car parking	10
Comfort and cleanliness	7
Scenery and surroundings	2
Staff attitude	7
Racecard and communication	5
Having a bet	7
Catering	9
Bars	7
Viewing and shelter	8

Total (out of 100) **70**
Ranked joint 29th out of 59

Hotels, pubs and restaurants
☆

other courses needing to maximise their revenue sources. Just as well it exists, too, because Wolverhampton is not overendowed with alternatives. The best recommendation is to travel a few miles towards Bridgnorth to the Old Vicarage at Worfield, for comfortable rooms and a decent restaurant. If you want to eat out near the course, you will find some of the best Indian restaurants around but not much else. The pubs here focus far less on dining than in most areas but there is some very good beer to be supped – notably the locally brewed Batham's bitter at the Great Western, behind the railway station, and a home-brew served at the Beacon at Sedgley, two miles south of town off the A4123.

• **TOP TIP**: Only come for the beer.

WORCESTER

The game is now afoot. With Areana Leisure in possession of a deal that will put it in control of racing's media lifeline, even the half-witted can understand the motives behind its predatory racecourse sctivity and admire the foresight of a company that recognised the way the sport must be financed and set about aquiring the largest possible stake, that puts it in effective control.

It is one thing, though, to admire cute business sense, quite another to admire Arena's racecourses. They are, to put it mildly, a rum bunch. Three all-weather tracks were bought for a specific

The parade ring and grandstand beyond looking southwards at Worcester.

purpose and serve it, however drearily; Windsor has its river setting and its Monday night crowds. But Folkestone and Worcester? Oh dear.

There may be grand plans for both these venues, probably including such lucrative add-ons as hotels, but just for now they offer the lowest level of spectator satisfaction to be found anywhere on the British racing circuit. Even in these enlightened times, that is saying something.

Worcester is the greater disappointment for I have fond memories of the place. Maybe it was always only just the right side of seedy but it had a solid, comfortable air. Now, the facilities have regressed alarmingly and the place no longer feels welcoming.

Things were so bad on my first inspection, a Saturday afternoon, that I returned for an evening fixture to make sure. The only improvement was a decrease in the number of beer-swilling undesirables who, on the Saturday, were allowed to lurch around the stands and concourses creating an atmosphere unpleasant to all

but the inebriate and rowdy. Where was the security? And how many decent patrons left with a vow to strike Worcester from their visiting list?

In truth, there were plenty of other causes to think that way. For reasons I have never been able to fathom, Worcester is invariably grid-locked on a Saturday afternoon. Nothing Arena can do about this, of course, but if it wants any kind of crowd in place before the second race perhaps it should devise – and signpost – a route around the city centre.

The next item on the job list should be the **car parks**, which are a disgrace. The access is across the course itself, which creates still further chaos once racing is under way, the surfaces are rough and prone to waterlogging, the stewarding haphazard. During 2001, visible improvements began.

With the possible exception of certain low-grade rugby league grounds in industrially impoverished areas, it is hard to think of another professional sports venue that creates such a dismal initial impression. And this, remember, in a privileged setting among peeping church spires on the banks of the River Severn.

Sadly, nothing improved at the entrance, where I wandered through a gate entirely unchecked. The Arena blazers, disproportionately conspicuous among the sparse all-weather crowds, were in short supply here.

At least there was a decent

Again looking southwards, the city of Worcester is to the left on the further side of the course.

racecard, priced at £1.50 and containing a track facts page of statistics relevant to the course, along with details of Arena's enterprising theme days and offers and a clear guide to the course facilities. This last item occupied more space than the facilities merited.

CATERING

I am not sure what has happened to Worcester's catering. There doesn't seem to be any, nowadays, at least none that can be recommended. I deliberately discount the fast-food wagons parked on the lawn, lazy catering that reflects no credit on the track.

There is a members' dining room, partitioned from a crowded bar on the first floor of the stand and looking backwards on to the river. There is a coffee bar that sells, er, coffee, and a snack bar downstairs that resembles the most hideous of 1970s' motorway cafes. And that's it.

The bars are no better and the one attempt at an outlet to match the summer programme

---

TRACK DETAILS

An oval-shaped course, 13 furlongs round, with easy left-handed turns.

---

now staged here fell horribly flat – a paddock bar was so laughably ill stocked and understaffed it would have shamed a village fête.

Worcester is a crumbling relic, with a stand that demands urgent refurbishment, a decrepit weighing-room building like a works canteen and an attitude of terminal decline. Arena must know all this. It is time something was done.

HOTELS, PUBS AND RESTAURANTS

Walk along the riverside from the course to the road bridge and, just the far side, stands Brown's Restaurant, the kind of place that identifies a town. The setting is wonderful and the food is pretty good, too – it is worth stressing

HOW TO GET THERE

By road: Racecourse is in the centre of Worcester, off the M5 (J6 or J7).
By rail: Walking distance from Worcester Foregate St, or by taxi from Worcester Shrub Hill.
Admission: Members £14, Tattersalls £10, centre course £5.

Website: www.worcester-race-course.co.uk

MARKS OUT OF TEN

Access	5
Car parking	3
Comfort and cleanliness	4
Scenery and surroundings	7
Staff attitude	5
Racecard and communication	8
Having a bet	6
Catering	3
Bars	5
Viewing and shelter	6

Total (out of 100) 52
Ranked 59th out of 59

Hotels, pubs and restaurants
☆☆☆

that it has nothing to do with the nationwide chain of brasseries. For years, this was the solitary restaurant in Worcester worth recommending but the dining scene in the town is sharpening up. Hotels here have always been a mixed bag and some of the best known have insultingly small rooms. The Diglis, further along the riverside from Brown's, has long been a personal favourite and the Star, in the centre of town, is a reasonable alternative. There is an increasing number of good dining pubs in the area, with the Kings Arms and Crown & Sandys Arms, neighbours in the tiny village of Ombersley, among the best. On the road to Stratford, the Coventry Arms at Upton Snodsbury is a rambling place with the large menu. Back in Worcester itself, the Cardinal's Hat is not only the town's oldest pub but serves some of the best beer around.

• **TOP TIP**: Brown's Restaurant.

YARMOUTH

Windy Shore and Ocean Dawn had the 'No Vacancies' signs up in their gaunt Victorian porches. Doubtless, it was something to do with Chubby Brown's eagerly awaited appearance at the Britannia Pier Theatre. The World's Largest Rock Shop had drawn a crowd but the late summer holidaymakers were resisting the lure of the new Posh and Becks models at the House of Wax and even the entreaties of Harriet Gipsy Lee ('Enter this door, worry no more').

Out past the Chic Shopping Arcade, which was anything but true to its name, and stroll along the sand dunes to the dubious delights of the Iron Duke public house, its adjoining caravan park and the gates of Yarmouth racecourse. Settings do not come much tackier than this.

As a county, Norfolk is bewitching, studded with village gems and fringed by a wonderfully unspoilt coastline. Yarmouth, its biggest town and, for some unfathomable reason, its biggest draw, belongs to another world, another age. And so does its racecourse. Nothing stylish, nothing smart, this is the course that time forgot.

It has its splashes of faded charm. There is a brightly coloured stewards' box with clocktower and an antique club stand, where the roof terrace offers the best view of racing and, as a bonus, peeps above the dunes to the North Sea. It is reasonably well supported, thanks to its captive summer audience. Given a hefty injection of investment and imagination, it could even present quite a thriving image. This, though, is a council-owned course, which is akin to having a red cross painted on its doors.

Brighton has been rescued from greater dilapidation by new ownership and progressive management but Yarmouth remains on the sick list. Steve Smith Eccles, who had his first and only flat ride here, reckons it has not changed since – and that is 27 years of steady decline.

Its position is a boon for Newmarket trainers, to whom the straight mile makes it almost a local nursery track, but a bane to everyone else. Train services are poor and the roads can be slow. In its favour are excellent AA signposts, skirting the town. The **car parks** are on grass and, at £2 per car, something of a liberty.

Racecards are sold by young women in smartly identifying yellow T-shirts, a plus offset by the price of £1.50 for a card that is well designed and subsidised by ample advertising but light on editorial content.

The Yarmouth course on the North Denes has a seaside atmosphere.

It is best not to make too close a study of the main stand, which from the rear resembles a prison block. The course can do little about its scenery – caravans to the fore, scrubland and bungalows behind – but it could surely try harder to brighten the image of its own buildings.

Fresh paint on some of the oldest structures speak of limited efforts, while the plentiful toilets boast bars of soap with 'Welcome' printed on them. It is as piecemeal as that. Bookmakers must hate it here – apart from the predominance of £1-each-way punters, they are obliged to make their primitive pitch on rough grass.

CATERING

The best of the homespun bars has a patio leading out to the buzzy paddock. There is a choice of wines, with Muscadet kept on ice, but the effect is spoilt in places by understaffing.

Apart from the absence of fresh coffee, the catering is surprisingly good. A marquee houses a carvery buffet, there is a members' seafood restaurant with a chummy, bistro feel and, below the Tattersalls stand, a shellfish bar where the smell of the sea permeates the building and local produce is well used.

The track here is flat and narrow, the ground rising to the stands affording easy viewing.

Between races, on an open bandstand, a Brylcreemed rock 'n' roll outfit bashed out some 1950s' classics. Somehow, it was in keeping with the feel of the place.

HOW TO GET THERE

By road: North of Great Yarmouth, signposted from the A47.
By rail: To Great Yarmouth, then bus or taxi to course.
Admission: Club £15, Tattersalls £9.50, Silver Ring £5.

Website: No official website.

MARKS OUT OF TEN

Access 7
Car parking 5
Comfort and cleanliness 5
Scenery and surroundings ... 4
Staff attitude 7
Racecard and
communication 6
Having a bet 4
Catering 7
Bars 7
Viewing and shelter 7

Total (out of 100) **59**
Ranked 55th out of 59

Hotels, pubs and restaurants
☆

TRACK DETAILS

A flat, oval, left-handed course, 13 furlongs in extent, with a run-in of 5 furlongs.

HOTELS, PUBS AND RESTAURANTS

The Seafood Restaurant on the north quay is a popular spot, not least among the Newmarket set, but Yarmouth itself offers precious little else that is not tacky or tawdry. So many hotels, so little class. Doubtless, it caters for a particular holiday market and may do so very well, but for a return to civilisation, head north up the coast to Winterton-on-Sea, where the Fisherman's Return has great views, fish meals, Woodforde's Wherry ale and is, on top of all that, a pleasant place to stay. Next to the beach at the appropriately named Horsey, the Nelson Head serves good beer and hearty pub food in an atmosphere as far removed from the horrors of Yarmouth as it is possible to imagine.

• **TOP TIP**: Leave town and head north.

YORK

The Knavesmire has come a long way since the times when a raceday was thought to be incomplete without a public execution as a sideshow. The gallows, where Dick Turpin was hanged in 1739, are still marked but these days this green and pleasant area is a monument to good taste.

York races had already settled here when Turpin met his end and there has been no cause to consider moving. The track is wide, flat

The Knavesmire at York still has something of its pastoral character.

York's older stands are richly decorated.

and devoid of excuses; the infrastructure has grown and adapted with the times until now it can be held up as the most attractive and efficient in the land.

Only fools and philistines would spurn the chance of a few days in this beguiling city, and the racecourse benefits from being within walking distance of the walled centre and a mere mile from the station that brings trains from London in 106 minutes.

Those who arrive by car may be deceived by the close-up of the course from the A64 dual carriageway, a road that actually has to be criss-crossed giddily before finding a way in. Regular signs allay panic, though, and the best landmark is the clocktower of the Terry's chocolate factory, gazing down like a relative fallen on hard times.

No such penury assails the racecourse. Its **parking** and traffic systems are as effective as can be contrived in a popular city setting, its entrance lobbies are businesslike and its welcome message emblazoned in yellow flowerbeds. Enter from the city end, along the distinctive tree-lined avenue, and the benches and thatched huts soothe like a walk in the park.

The weighing-room is a Georgian delight, the pavilioned champagne bar the loveliest of its kind on any British racecourse and even the judge's box has a thatched roof and flowers draped around its midriff. York, though, cannot be accused of that political buzzword of the moment, 'froth'; it has substance with its style.

249

TRACK DETAILS

York is a left-handed course, 2 miles in extent. It is flat throughout, and provides a fair test to all types of horses.

CATERING

They charge £40 for club badges in Ebor week, with 16–23 year olds enterprisingly at half price, so certain standards must be expected. The stately County Stand provides them in full, from the coveted Gimcrack dining rooms to the snug alcoves in the bars and the exemplary viewing on several levels. Up on the fourth floor, a lovingly tended racing museum has an adjoining tearoom that might have been transported down from the Shambles.

You also need a County Stand badge to enter quintessential York, the outdoor seafood and champagne bars on the terrace and lawns above the parade ring. This is the spot to spend those lazy, hazy days of summer. If only they dispensed something better than instant coffee, it would be perfect.

Perhaps the best thing about York is that its newest, ritziest facility stands classlessly in Tattersalls. The Knavesmire Stand, opened four years ago, is a four-tier affair which puts most of its competitors to shame. There are smart bars everywhere, all branded on racehorse names, and a self-service restaurant for which queues can form two hours before racing.

York endears itself further by refusing to impose the rip-off

HOW TO GET THERE

By road: The course is on the Knavesmire Road to the south of the city, and can be accessed via the A19 and the A64.
By rail: To York, then bus or taxi.
Admission: County Stand £20–£40, Tattersalls £10–£20, course £4–£5 (prices vary depending on meeting).

Website: www.yorkracecourse.co.uk

prices with which smugly misguided managements routinely alienate patrons all round the country. You can spend £78 on Dom Perignon if you wish but the house champagne sells at under £20, decent wine from £9 to £15 a bottle and bitter at £2.14 a pint.

There are relics, here, of a bygone age, none better than the benched terrace in front of the oldest stand, overhung by elaborate ironwork, its pillars hooped in red, white and blue as if to advertise a massive barber's shop. Hangings apart, York has not abandoned its heritage, but neither has it missed a beat of the march of progress.

MARKS OUT OF TEN	
Access	7
Car parking	8
Comfort and cleanliness	9
Scenery and surroundings	7
Staff attitude	8
Racecard and communication	9
Having a bet	7
Catering	8
Bars	10
Viewing and shelter	9
Total (out of 100)	**82**

Ranked 1st out of 59

Hotels, pubs and restaurants
☆ ☆ ☆ ☆ ☆

HOTELS, PUBS AND RESTAURANTS

Not just a wholly distinguished racecourse but a delightful city for everything social. Though the pubs are plentiful, the action tends centre on the innumerable fine hotels in the area. Middlethorpe Hall actually overlooks the course and, if you can afford it, is a mighty fine base, while the Grange, close to the city centre, is a Regency town house with a renowned restaurant. My personal favourite is in Fulford – hence very handy for the racecourse – where the York Pavilion has rooms in the main house and in converted stables set around a charming courtyard, and the brasserie-style restaurant is outstanding.

- **TOP TIP**: The York Pavillion Hotel for food and lodging.